GET A Love LIFE

Michelle McKinney Hammond

HARVEST HOUSE PUBLISHERS
Eugene, Oregon 97402

Cover by Koechel Peterson & Associates, Minneapolis, Minnesota

GET A LOVE LIFE
Copyright © 2000 by Michelle McKinney Hammond
Published by Harvest House Publishers
Eugene, Oregon 97402

Library of Congress Cataloging-in-Publication Data
McKinney Hammond, Michelle, 1957-
   Get a love life / Michelle McKinney Hammond
     p. cm.
   ISBN 0-7369-0186-8
   1. God—Worship and love. I. Title
   BV4817 .M38 1999
   231'.6—dc21   99-042962

This one is for the One who loves me most. Lord, my heart burns for You. It is my determination to keep the flame high.

Acknowledgments

To my wonderful parents,

Mr. & Mrs. George & Charity Hammond
Mr. & Mrs. William & Norma McKinney
*You have taught me what love looks
like by your example.*

To my Harvest House Family,
*you continue to inspire me with your
wonderfulness. I love you.*

To Steve Miller,
thanks for keeping me honest!

To all my buds and sisters—you know who you are.
*Your unconditional love means more
to me by the minute.*

ontents

1

How's Your Love Life?

From the moment she entered the restaurant I could tell something was different about Shirley. She'd changed since the last time we had gotten together. The girl was literally vibrating as she bounced into the room. Others must have sensed it, too, because heads turned to follow her progress as she made her way toward my table. I noticed that the majority of her observers were men. And who could blame them? Not only did she look as sharp as a tack in her cream-colored designer suit, Shirley literally glowed! She radiated joy and contentment. Truly, all was well in her world. She slid into the seat opposite me, looking very pleased with herself, and pulled up her chair, landing both elbows on the table and leaning in toward me for effect.

"So, what's new with you?" she said. Immediately I knew she was asking this question simply to be polite. That much was obvious. From the Cheshire cat grin on her face, she was literally bursting at the seams to tell me something exciting. Although all the obvious signs made Shirley's news amusingly apparent, I purposed not to ruin her fun by guessing aloud what she was dying to tell me. To tell you the truth, I rather enjoyed watching her squirm as she waited for me to finish my list of catch-up notes. Finally, when I knew she couldn't hold back her news any longer, I eased her blood pressure by asking, "So, how's your love life?"

"It is absolutely fabulous!" she purred, the excitement in her voice reminding me of a car in high idle. In fact, if she had been a vehicle, I think she would have jump-started right there on the spot and run over me. From across the table I could feel her heart racing at the mere thought of the new man in her life. "Girl, this is it!" she said, shifting her position for emphasis. "I have finally met HIM!"

Oooh, this was serious. HIM was not to be confused with merely *him*. This was final. I felt a little envious as Shirley began her dissertation on all the points that had caused her to conclude that this definitely was HIM. He was this; he was that. Oh! And by the way, he was all of that and more. He was the most gorgeous man she had ever seen in her life. On that note she whipped out a picture of HIM for me to see. He was all right in my estimation, nothing to write home about, yet he was everything to her. Needless to say our entire lunch was filled with HIM. Every word he spoke was the essence of brilliance, and everything he did was, well, you get the picture. And when we actually weren't talking about HIM, I could tell from her distant eyes and feeble attempts to pretend she was listening to my words that her mind was still on HIM.

After we had finished lunch and gone our separate ways, I felt as if I had a HIM hangover. I shook my head, chuckling to myself, "Wow! That's some kind of love." I thought of my own life as a single woman and how many times I have been addressed with that same question: "How's your love life?" There have been times when I've been quick to answer, "I don't have one." But lately my answer has changed. I, like my girlfriend Shirley, now find myself answering with a smile on my face, "It is just simply divine."

I Feel Love

Divine indeed! Because my love interest is not just any man. This man is a lover like no other; he loves me down to my very soul! I know he has millions of other women, yet he makes me feel as if I am the only one. And though I know I have to share him with others, I don't mind because he is always available when I need him. He's generous, thoughtful, sensitive, wise, strong, consistent, faithful, true, and always keeps his promises. And, on top of all of that, he is the fairest of ten thousand. Yes, you guessed it; the lover of my soul is Jesus. We've got a love thing going on! As I began to share this with some of my friends, their expressions ranged from a quiet knowing to envy to complete befuddlement. This was when I realized that many Christians, though quick to say that they love the Lord, are not acquainted with the concept nor the experience of truly being *in* love with Him. There is a difference between *loving* and being *in love*. And the balance between the two can create a serious deficit in a relationship. This is where many marriages fall apart.

One of my favorite poems is by the French poet Jacques Prevert. It narrates the early morning breakfast of a married couple from the wife's point of view. It is a mournful tale of her loneliness as she watches her husband go through the motions of preparing a cup of coffee, smoking a cigarette, and putting on his hat and raincoat as he prepares to go out into the morning. As she systematically lists his every move, she punctuates each action with the words, "without looking at me, without speaking to me." Poor woman! Can you imagine what it would be like to live in a home with someone who did not even acknowledge your presence? And this couple was French! If you know anything about the French, the mavens of romance, you know that they didn't start off that way. If that were the case, they never would have made it to the marriage altar.

    As I pondered how a marriage could deteriorate to such a pitiful state of affairs with two people living together in such a sorry fashion, a thought hit me. I realized God could write this same poem about His relationship with many of us. As Christians we make up the body of the bride of Christ. If the truth were told, most of us are in a pretty dry marriage with our Savior. We, like young honeymooners, were in a state of bliss when we first came to the Lord. Do you remember that time? Couldn't get enough of reading the Word. Beat the pastor to the church for every service and Bible class. Couldn't stop witnessing and inviting even your enemies to church. Mmm hmm, I knew you could relate to what I was talking about. But then something happened. Somewhere along the way we lost our passion. We decided we just didn't need to make all of that effort. It was time to "exercise wisdom." Like those who settle into a marriage and decide there is no more need to date, that the money would best be saved for the mortgage, we concluded that we should be practical about spiritual things. We didn't want to be accused of being fanatical or obsessed with this Jesus thing. So we calmed down and became more pragmatic about our newfound faith.

We got down to the business of Christianity, learned the rules of the game, mastered the language, got in the right sanctified circles, and concentrated on "arriving." We started going through the motions of being good little saved do-bees—*doing* everything right instead of *being* who God has called us to be—worshippers. Worshipping Him in spirit and in truth—now that's true intimacy. But we became "religious" and forgot about the relationship we were supposed to be having with Him. Kinda like the Ephesian church in the book of Revelation.

I know your deeds and your toil and perseverance, and that you cannot endure evil men, and you put to the test those who call themselves apostles, and they are not, and you found them to be false; and you have perseverance and have endured for My name's sake, and have not grown weary. But I have this against you, that you have left your first love.
—Revelation 2:2-4 NASB

How could God have something against a group of people who were doing so many things right? It's the same way a man feels when he goes in search of a mistress when his wife is too busy being the perfect mother, housekeeper, and cook to show him any affection. God's heart longs for the praise that He so rightfully deserves.

Hello, Is It Me You're Looking For?

I think that if God were to rewrite the Jacques Prevert poem to let us know how He felt it would go something like this: "Last night I watched you sleep, anticipating the morning when I could share My heart with you. But when you awoke you headed straight for the bathroom without speaking to Me, without acknowledging Me. So I waited for you. I waited for you to finish your morning routine, thinking we would have some time together then. While you sipped your coffee, I could share with you from My Word. But you read the morning paper instead without speaking to Me, without acknowledging Me. I watched you as you went on your way, and I longed to prepare you for the events of the day. But you flipped on your cell phone and visited with a friend on your way to work without acknowledging Me. So I waited for you to take your morning coffee break, our next window of opportunity for a quiet moment together. But you sought out a coworker instead to chat with and pass the time. Well, the lunch break came and went, with you busying yourself with errands and idle chatter with passersby. And still you had no time for Me. I settled into waiting for the end of the day for us to unwind and spend time together. But you filled your evening with preparing dinner, completing household chores, conversing with friends and family. Without speaking to Me. Without acknowledging Me. And as you watched the evening news and wondered aloud what the world was coming to, I longed to tell you, but your comments were not addressed to Me. Eventually you made your way to your bedroom. There, in the stillness of the dark, My desire to embrace you and tell you how much I love you was overwhelming. But you climbed into bed, fell against the pillow voicing your exhaustion, and fell asleep without speaking to Me, without ever acknowledging Me."

Can I get a witness to this scene? We all do this at some time or another. Some of us do it far too often. We feel chagrin when we finally acknowledge how shoddy our prayer life is, yet many of us never apply ourselves to doing anything to fix it. And we fool ourselves into thinking that if perhaps we could see Him, things would be different.

Where Is the Love?

Let's face it. For the most part, the church is a weary, bored spouse, too busy going through the meaningless motions of Christianity to have a deep relationship with the Lord. Our passion for the Lord, the Lover of Our Souls, is gone—if we ever had that passion in the first place. The flame that once ignited our hearts has dwindled down to cold embers as we get down to what we deem more practical issues—how to run our churches, how to take care of our families, how to live our lives. We think we know all the tricks to getting what we want from God. Straining under the weight of crossing our theological it's and dotting our spiritual it's, we have forgotten one very important fact—we don't have to work so hard. We *have* a relationship with God. Based on relationship, He moves on our behalf. If the church could ever get hold of the enormity of this one revelation, a whole lot of churches and ministries would have to refocus their emphasis; otherwise, they would be empty.

How to increase our faith. How to get healing. How to get deliverance. How to get wealth. And on and on and on. We have a course for just about everything these days. Men and women in Bible times had access to none of these classes, yet God showed up and blessed them with abundance, with healing, with manifestations of miracles and power. As a matter of fact, I would dare to say that they saw God more than we see Him today. Why? Because they simply chose to believe God rather than manipulate Him by twisting His arm behind His Word. They had no programs or seminars; all they had was a relationship to go on—a relationship with Him.

A relationship gives us experiences to draw from that frame the reality of someone else's level of caring for us.

Based on the evidence that person gives us, we either sing his praises or curse the day we allowed him into our lives. And this is where the whole love thing gets murky. What it takes to set one person's heart on fire wouldn't make the next person blink. Yet a true lover knows what it takes to move the soul of his love. God is the consummate lover. He knows what it takes to fill you with shivers of delight. He knows what to do, but either we don't recognize His touch or we don't have a clue how to respond.

As I broached the subject of falling in love with God with several of my friends, they all drew blanks. Certainly they *loved* God, but they had to confess that they were not *in love* with Him. How to make that happen was an even more perplexing question. Love is the great intangible, is it not? My friend Shirley was madly in love with someone who was of no romantic interest to me. Her love for this man was based on what wonderful things he did for her and how special he made her feel when they were together. As I began to ask my Christian friends about the things God did for them, including how He made them feel when they really got serious about spending quality time with Him, they seemed amazed at the things they had taken for granted. So many times they had overlooked God's hand in the process.

Making a Love Connection

Perhaps the great dilemma here is how to love someone we cannot see. Crossing the chasm of the invisible and the divine is a major disconnect for most people. God is up there and we are down here. God is so much larger than anything we can imagine that the concept of embracing Him in mortal terms eludes us. Yet this is the secret to falling in love with God. Translating what we already know and relate to from the natural into the spiritual is an experience that will light our hearts and renew our minds.

As my friends began to query me on how I had come to the place of falling in love with Jesus, I found myself at a loss as to how to explain it. How do you explain how to fall in love with someone? "I just did," was my first response. But then I had to admit that I did have my reasons for such an answer. I looked for God in everything—in every encounter, in every circumstance. Good or bad, I tracked Him down in the middle of it. I compare it to when tourists visit Hollywood. They become consumed with spotting the rich and famous on every corner, and eventually they do see someone. I believe we have to look for God in that very way. And when we seek Him, we find Him.

I must arise now and go about the city; In the streets and in the squares I must seek *him whom my soul loves.*
—Song of Solomon 3:2 NASB, emphasis mine

But from there you will seek *the LORD your God, and you will find Him if you search for Him with all your heart and all your soul.*
—Deuteronomy 4:29 NASB, emphasis mine

For me, seeking God in all things is a must. Shortly after I came to Christ, I was at a crossroads in my life. I could choose to live as a Christian or I could go the way of the world. It was a difficult decision because being godly was not working for me at the beginning. It was a joyless existence. I still loved the world and the things of it more than I loved my Heavenly Father, and I openly admitted this to

Him. I knew I either had to love Him or die. It was just that simple. If I didn't love Him, I would not be able to do what was required to please His heart. No pleasing His heart, no peace for my soul. That was the situation.

No servant can serve two masters; *for either he will hate the one, and love the other, or else he will hold to one, and despise the other.*
—Luke 16:13 NASB, emphasis mine

I knew that the state of my heart toward God would be my key to victory or failure as a Christian. This is an important concept to understand. If we're all honest with ourselves, we must admit that love is the motivating factor for everything we do. Our passion for our spouse, our job, or our home becomes the motivation for how much effort we put into doing what it takes to maintain these things. When we don't love our jobs, we tend not to put much effort into them. When we don't love our homes, we are not very fussy about their upkeep. When we don't love our spouses, we avoid them, missing the little cues that alert us to their needs, and the relationship dies a slow and painful death right before our eyes. When we don't fall in love with God, we find ourselves constantly striving for someone or something else to fill that gap in our souls. And because no earthly thing or person can fill a God-sized void, we end up settling in the land of the discontent, disgruntled with God and angry with ourselves for not being able to make this "Christian thing" work. After all, now that we know God, aren't we supposed to be happy?

Perhaps that's what Adam was thinking in the garden. Everything was perfect enough, yet something was missing.

So God concluded that it was not good for man to be alone. But Adam wasn't really alone. God walked with him in the cool of the evening daily in the garden. Yet God stated that Adam was alone. Even Adam himself couldn't put his finger on what exactly was awry. But God knew there was a level of fellowship that Adam had not yet experienced. Adam had been made in God's image, yet he was not one with God. He only reflected the soul of God. Therefore, he had not been privy to the experience of being "one" with someone. God knew the oneness of the Trinity. He understood the intimacy of being a part of another, but this understanding had completely escaped Adam. Even in his magnificent fellowship with God, man could only go so far.

So God created Eve. Knowing Eve intimately would give Adam a new understanding of how to fellowship with God on a deeper level, spirit to spirit, even as he connected to Eve body to body. But then came the fall of Adam and Eve. They turned toward one another and away from God. When they took their hearts out of God's hands, life became hard. Eve would now have a difficult labor in childbirth, and Adam would have to toil hard to make a living. They would even have to work at maintaining their love for one another. Where did our love for God go? The world stole it.

...the woman who is unmarried, and the virgin, is concerned about the things of the Lord, that she may be holy both in body and spirit; but one who is married is concerned about the things of the world, how she may please her husband.

—1 Corinthians 7:34 NASB, emphasis mine

Everyone on the face of the earth longs to be loved and to give love. God made us that way on purpose, hoping that we would turn to Him and revel in the fullness of His love. But He realized that we needed something that showed us what intimacy should feel like, so He created human relationships as the example. These relationships, however, were never designed to replace the love relationship we were created to have with Him. Whether you're single or not, my question to you is this: Who are you married to—God or the world? The world is a difficult husband. It is demanding, ungracious, and selfish. And life with someone who doesn't love you back is hard.

God, however, is a loving partner, pouring out countless benefits and lavishing us with constant reminders of His care for us. So how do we get in on all those wonderful blessings? How do we get back on the road to loving Him according to His original design? How do we leave the labor of being a Christian behind and get back to the good life? It's actually easier than you think. If you're up to the challenge, I dare you to get a love life with God.

On the Love Tip: First Things First

My first suggestion is that you make a list of all the characteristics you would like to have in a spouse. This is going to call for some digging beneath the surface, past good-looking and a sharp dresser. (You can, however, throw in wealthy because that does apply to God.) Mainly, though, I'm talking about heart qualities, the things that really matter through the long haul. Now look at that list and look for God. Isn't He everything that you put on your list? Next go back through a day in your life and list all of the things God did for you through others, things that were a help and a blessing to you. Remember, never take anything for granted! Never chalk anything up to mere circumstance. You need to start seeing God meeting you everywhere, speaking to you through every kind word, touching you in every pleasant encounter. Breathe out a "thank you" for those special and priceless moments, no matter how fleeting they were, and feel the embers in your heart beginning to stir. That's it! You're on your way to getting a love life!

————————————————

Love Note

From God's heart to yours...
I have loved you with an everlasting love;
therefore I have drawn you with lovingkindness.

————————————————

2
Love Talk

hirley bolted upright from her relaxed position as the phone interrupted our afternoon together. "Hello? Oh, hi!" That was all I needed to hear to know that it was HIM. My girlfriend's voice had changed and taken on a timbre I had never heard before. And as she proceeded to coo and giggle for no apparent reason, I thought to myself, *Funny, she never talks to me that way.* I watched her settle into her chair, eyes aglow, wriggling around as if wrapping herself in a cozy blanket to prepare for a long, warm conversation. On that note I held up a sanctified finger as if excusing myself in the middle of a church sermon and let myself out. No way was I going to compete with HIM for her attention. I knew I had been effectively dismissed when she didn't even acknowledge my rising to go. She was totally focused on HIM. Her attention would not and could not be divided. Although she couldn't see HIM, it was enough for her to listen to his voice. "I just love talking to him," she had sighed in earlier conversation. "The more I learn about him, the more I love him." She related this to me with that faraway look in her eyes that I was beginning to grow accustomed to at the mere mention of HIM. "He's just so...you know..." I didn't, but that was quite all right with me; I didn't need to know anything about HIM. He was *her* man.

But Shirley did make me pause and reflect on my own love relationship with the Lord. Did I feel the same way about talking to God? Did I look forward to my quiet time with Him? Did I long to hear His voice? I concluded that loving God was crucial to having a healthy prayer life. After all, prayer is conversation. It is intimate fellowship. And God desires to have both with us. This is why we were created—to share and exchange with Him.

Thou art worthy, O Lord, to receive glory and honour and power: for thou hast created all things, and for thy pleasure *they are and were created.*

—Revelation 4:11 KJV, emphasis mine

Let's return to the garden for a moment. The Lord came down there daily to walk and talk with Adam in the cool of the evening. This brought pleasure to His heart. What did they find to talk about? Anything and everything, I'm sure. As God related stories of creation and the plans He had for man, it is safe to assume that Adam had a million questions. They had an exchange going on there, a dialogue between man and God. Heaven and earth met, uniting the spiritual and the natural, completing the picture of God's omniscient inspiration. This was fellowship on a whole different level from what had previously occurred in the heavenlies. In the garden, friendship was mingled with worship, and a divine love affair was conceived.

My thoughts shifted back to Shirley. Shirley was not normally a phone person. She did not dilly-dally around on the phone until she met HIM. Now she was on that thing for hours at a time! Why? Because Girlfriend was in love. If she couldn't see HIM, she had to talk to HIM. First thing in the morning. Right before she went to sleep at night. In the middle of the day. And not necessarily for any reason; just simply because. If he just wanted to sit and breathe on the phone, I'm sure that would have been all right with her, which makes my point as blatant as a neon sign. The time we spend talking to God is in direct correlation to how much we love Him. How much we love Him is affected by how much we know about Him. What does He think about this? How does He feel about that? And, more specifically, how does He feel about you and your personal circumstances? The more you know about someone, the more subjects you can discuss with that person. So we need to know as much as we can about our Heavenly Father.

Getting to Know You

Sitting across the table from a new male acquaintance, I studied his face. He looked like a nice man, but I was at a loss for words in our initial meeting. Mutual friends had introduced us. They sang his praises as they filled me in on all they knew about him. He was nice, had a good job, traveled a bit, liked art and music, was a sound Christian, active in his church, was looking for a wife.... You know, the broad-strokes description list. All of that sounded good, but I still didn't have enough specifics to immediately launch into a deep conversation with this guy. So after polite, surface greetings, I found myself simply waiting for him to say something that I could latch on to.

"So, tell me about yourself." He served up the standard fare of two strangers meeting. I never know where to begin when faced with that request. What about me would he like to know? As I hemmed and hawed, he helped me out. "I hear you like to travel. Where have you been?" As I began to list the places I liked most, a light went on in his eyes; we had something in common! We both loved Paris. He hadn't been to Africa but wanted to go. "What kind of music do you like?" I queried. He responded that he enjoyed easy listening, jazz, classic singers, contemporary gospel, good worship songs. Hmm...now things were looking up. Next I asked him what areas of ministry he was involved in at his church and what speakers and authors he liked. Now we were off and running. We were definitely on the same page on many issues and preferences. Needless to say, after three hours of nonstop conversation, the dinner meeting was a resounding success. We promised to get together sooner rather than later to continue our intriguing discussion!

Funny what a little information can do. For so many, prayer time with our Father is not as juicy as my above-mentioned exchange with a total stranger. It is a time of dry, one-sided conversation that consists of us submitting to God a list of anxieties and requests. Yet prayer needs to be more than that. Prayer is essential when it comes to nurturing our love for God. Intimate interchange is what stirs the embers of the heart. I recall the times when I've poured out my heart to God about something that was weighing heavily upon my emotions. As I sat waiting to hear His response, I felt the need to read a specific portion of Scripture. When I turned to it, the verses said precisely what I needed to hear. And I began to weep, so overwhelmed was I that God would choose such a sweet way to show me that

He knows exactly how I feel. That He is concerned about the way I take. That He has heard me and is going to do something about my need. Yes, prayer is supposed to be a *two-way* conversation! We must press past this idea of God being merely a cosmic ball of light up in the sky, so lofty and untouchable that we pay Him lip service only to appease Him and then go on our way. No! God wants to talk to us. He wants to hear what we have to say, and He wants to respond to us!

Heart to Heart

I find it significant that the Lord chose to come down to the garden to visit Adam. He didn't send a heavenly elevator to earth to export Adam up to the cosmos. Nor did He make Adam look up to the sky to talk with Him. No, He came down to walk and talk with Adam—heart to heart. And though we must reverence Him as the awesome God that He is, we must realize that God also desires the loving exchange that a father has with his sons and daughters. He wants you to climb up in His lap, put your arms around Him, and tell Him how you feel. Then He will rock you and give you words of comfort and instruction. He wants to give you a gentle squeeze and let you know that everything is going to be all right because He said so. Remember how much better your mother or father could make you feel when they did that? Suddenly the world would be okay again because you had the assurance that Mommy or Daddy was going to fix it.

Despite God's great love for us, prayer is boring to many. But I've got to tell you something here: Prayer is only boring when *you* are boring. Sorry, I thought you knew! God is always interesting, so it's up to us to make our part of the conversation interesting. Think about it in mortal terms. How do you feel when you are speaking with people who won't let you get a word in edgewise? Who talk incessantly about themselves? Who constantly repeat themselves? Who reiterate information you already knew? Or what about those people who talk to you, yet their attention is divided? And let's not even mention the people who only call you up when they want something. Doesn't that just irk you to no end? And when they go over the top and begin to whine and beg for effect, don't you just want to scream? Well, how do you think God feels when we do the same things to Him?

A lot of these bad habits are born out of religion and must be disposed of if we are going to have any type of an enjoyable relationship with God. Think about it. Does the following sound familiar? "Father God, this" and "Father God, that" and "Father God, this, that, and the other." Or "Lord, this" and "Lord, that" and "Lord, this too." No one talks like that when they are having a normal conversation! No one repeats the person's name ten times in the same sentence. The other person listening would think you had a problem. You repeat his name for emphasis on a specific point, yes, but inadvertently peppering the entire dialogue with his name would make him crazy. I call it fill-in-the-blank prayer.

Another bad habit is composing longwinded, elaborate prayers. We may think we are impressing God, but we aren't. Every word we say should be a word that counts and comes from the heart. Jesus warned us against lengthy prayers that are nothing more than vain repetition:

And when you are praying, do not use meaningless repetition, *as the Gentiles do, for they suppose that* *they will be heard for their many words.*

—Matthew 6:7 NASB, emphasis mine

Another religious thing that's in style these days is shouting. Let's clear this up once and for all. Talk to God; shout at the devil. That's who you should be mad at. Intensity of voice that comes from passion is one thing, but shouting is quite another.

Surely the arm of the LORD is not too short to save, nor his ear too dull to hear.
—Isaiah 59:1 NIV, emphasis mine

People only shout when they think the person they are speaking to is too far away to hear or is not getting the point. But we don't need to shout at God. He says that He will draw near to us if we draw near to Him (James 4:8). He is that Someone who truly understands.

For we do not have a high priest who is unable to sympathize with our weaknesses, but we have one who has been tempted in every way, just as we are—yet was without sin.
—Hebrews 4:15 NIV

Jesus not only hears what we're saying; He feels it. But here is where love versus religious practice comes in to play. Remember Shirley, who I left as she was cooing on the phone? I knew whom she was talking to because of her tone of voice. Our voices, too, should reflect to whom we are speaking. I have nothing nice to say to the devil, so when I am in warfare prayer I speak with authority. I might shout, or simply speak firmly, but with him my tone is never friendly. When I talk to the Lord, however, my voice changes. It is filled with love, adoration, and appreciation for His goodness. As I enter into worship, my voice is filled with awe at His might, His power, His majesty. When I am telling Him my troubles, my tone changes to that of one speaking to a confidante and friend. It might intensify if I am upset or questioning something, but it does not rise to a full-blown shout unless I am shouting the victory. Hallelujah! Now that's something to shout about. You don't shout at a boyfriend, husband, or someone you cherish, so please don't shout at the Lord.

Doesn't it seem like people sometimes give unnecessary commentary and details that God already knows about when they are praying in public? They're saying these things for the benefit of those who are praying in agreement with them. I always imagine God saying, "Enough already! I know all of that; would you please get to the point?" I recommend giving the others the details *before* you begin to pray, then focusing on the solution when you take the issue to God. That is, if you want to be effective in prayer. If you just want to posture for those present, that's a different story.

One of the reasons we ramble on and on in prayer is because our concentration is divided. We are not focused. We are not listening to ourselves speak. Have you ever gotten perturbed at someone you were speaking to on the phone because you knew they were watching television, yelling at the kids, or maybe even on the computer while they were talking to you? Kinda made you feel that you were not very important in the scheme of things, didn't it? If you're anything like me, you probably threatened to hang up on the spot if the person didn't give you his or her undivided attention. Well, God is a jealous lover. And justifiably so after all He has done for us. He deserves our full regard.

Do not worship any other god, for the LORD, *whose
name is* Jealous, *is a* jealous God.

—Exodus 34:14 NIV, emphasis mine

For the LORD *your* God *is a consuming fire, a*
jealous God.

—Deuteronomy 4:24 NIV, emphasis mine

The Look of Love

God with a small "g" doesn't just fall under the heading
of idol worship. It alludes to anything you find more important than God—money, food, material possessions, a loved
one...you know what I mean. God wants to consume us
with His love. When Moses went into the Tent of Meetings
to meet with God, the cloud came down and covered the
entrance, blocking off everything else. But after the tabernacle was built with the articles of the Tent of Meetings
within, the cloud settled on the tent and the glory of God
filled the tabernacle. Moses was consumed by the presence
of God. No evil could penetrate that place because God surrounded it. God wants to surround our hearts like that.
When we spend time with Him, caught up in the rapture of
His love for us, consumed by His Spirit and His thoughts, it
shows. When Moses came down from the mountain where
He had been communing with God for forty days, his face
literally glowed. The Israelites needed sunglasses to look at
him! They didn't have any back then, of course, so they put
a veil over his face instead. Now that's intense. God and His
Word had been Moses' only focus, and as a result he was sat-
urated through and through with God.

When we spend our time in prayer totally focused on
God, determined to listen as well as talk, we enter into a
place of deep, all-consuming intimacy, the kind that

rearranges our hearts, renews our minds, and transforms our lives. There is no way the change won't show on our faces. Others will notice a difference in our countenance when we step out into the world. We will exude peace, joy, and fulfillment because of the things God has shared with us in secret. That's the daily bread Jesus was talking about when He taught the disciples to pray. Give me what I need to make it through this day, Lord, and we'll worry about tomorrow when we get to it. Give me the word and the instruction I need to deal with the issues at hand with a sound mind and a calm spirit. This is why it is crucial to pray daily. The landscape of our lives is constantly changing. Yesterday's directions could land us in a whole different neighborhood today. We've got to get fresh marching orders from God, who has a bird's-eye view of our situation. This is why He tells us that His steadfast love never ceases, that His mercies never come to an end. He's serving them up fresh and new every morning (Lamentations 3:23). He knows that love needs to be refreshed daily. Therefore, He leaves us needing just enough so that we will return to Him regularly. Many a single woman could take a lesson from God in this area when it comes to dealing with a romantic prospect.

Ed Cole, one of the fathers of the men's movement, does an incredible job teaching what it takes to keep a marriage alive. I have simplified his teachings into what I call the cycle of human love relationships from conception to deterioration by breaking it down into four levels. First is the *revelation*, or birthing, of the relationship. It's when we meet and are initially interested in each other. We are willing to take risks at this point in order to find the right method to secure the other person's interest. Once we've gotten their attention, we move to the *formalization* stage where the relationship is solidified. But once that happens, the relationship or marriage reaches the stage of *institutionalization*. The methods we once employed for love points have now become traditions. The course has been plotted and things are now done to secure the efficiency of the union. The concern for effectively rousing and sustaining interest is over. This is the danger zone because if you don't do something at this stage to keep the relationship fresh, it moves to the next level—*crystallization*. You become hard; nothing moves you. You are at a stalemate. Tradition has stifled creativity. No more impromptu trysts. No more impulsive gifts. No sweet nothings whispered in the dark. The thrill is gone. This is when someone in the relationship begins looking elsewhere in order to feel good all over again. And stupid moves are made that destroy the relationship forever.

God doesn't want that to happen in our relationship with Him, so He invites us into His presence for fresh romance every day. He knows that love has to be continually nurtured between two lovers; otherwise the flame goes out. This is why daily fellowship with God is so important, digging into His heart, finding out what's on His mind concerning you, the world, and His kingdom. Intimacy grows when we share private and secret things with one another, and that's exactly what God wants to do with us. He wants to whisper some things to us, give us some assurances, love on us before the world outside our door attempts to bruise us. His love can insulate us from the arrows the enemy of our soul throws our way. But, as is the nature of humans, we only look forward to talking to those we know and love. And if we don't know Him, it's hard to love and talk to Him.

Love on My Mind

Let me share a few things with you to set your heart on fire. Did you know that you are constantly on the mind of God?

---

*How precious to me are your thoughts, O God! How
vast is the sum of them! Were I to count them, they
would outnumber the grains of sand. When I awake,
I am still with you.*
                                        —Psalm 139:17 NIV

Talk about having love on your mind! I like that in a
man, don't you? The Lord longs after us; He wants to show
us through His graciousness how much He loves us (Isaiah
30:18). He longs to tell you secrets as you press into His
heart (Amos 3:7). He longs to reveal Himself to you and to
me as He truly is in all of His glory. Isn't that just precious?

When Jesus prayed in the Garden of Gethsemane, He
said something that really touches my heart. He said,
"Father, I want those you have given me to be with me
where I am, and to see my glory, the glory you have given
me because you loved me before the creation of the world"
(John 17:24 NIV). Wow! I am able to relate to that statement.

As I pondered what was on Jesus' heart when He said
that, I was reminded of a time in my own life several years
ago. I had lost my job due to cutbacks at the ad agency
where I worked. I moved to Los Angeles and fell on hard
times. I was unable to find a job, my unemployment ran
out, my savings dwindled to nothing, my car broke down,
and I was served an eviction notice for my apartment. My
new friends who were privy to all my misfortune had
difficulty swallowing the stories I told them of better days.
I would talk about the glamorous life I'd lived in Chicago,
staying in the finest of hotels, hobnobbing with the elite,
eating in fabulous restaurants, being on the best invitation
lists, and producing major money national commercials.
They couldn't imagine it. They just knew me as plain ole

broke, so they would politely nod and chalk up my conversation to delusions of grandeur.

Well, the following year I got my job back and returned to Chicago. You should have just seen my friends' faces when I flew out to L.A. for a production and took them to dinner, then whisked off to the Grammy Awards. You could have knocked them over with a feather! I then flew one of my friends to Chicago to visit me for her birthday, and when she saw my apartment she had to admit she needed to repent for thinking I was making up stories about my past when I lived in L.A. I now had a beautiful home and the blessings of God were apparent in my life. God had restored me and my friends were now witnessing me experiencing the American Dream, or whatever you want to call it. Personally, I call it occupying the promise—living and experiencing God's love.

But let's get back to Jesus here. Based on my memory, I imagine Him thinking that He had walked with these disciples and mentored them in the things of God for three years. He had never owned a home, had worn the same linen suit for as long as He could remember, had literally lived by faith and the hand of God, and that was all His followers could see. They had no concept of who really walked in their midst. No idea at all. Their earthly imaginations would never be able to grasp the concept of Jesus on a throne surrounded by angels singing His praises twenty-four, seven. No, this was beyond their scope of comprehension. He longed for them to see Him as He truly was. He was excited for them to see heaven, the magnificent place He had prepared for them. Not so much to puff Himself up, but so that they could finally see a better way, a place beyond where they currently lived bound by the finiteness of their limited existence.

Jesus knew that once the disciples got a glimpse of the reality of God's power, the breadth of His reach, the awesomeness of His magnificence, nothing would be impossible for them. He wanted to take them to another level in their faith so that they, too, could be overcomers rising above the visible to take hold of the victory that is hidden in the invisible. Because let's face it. At the end of the day, admiration does help push the needle on the love meter. By now you should know that love is the force behind the kind of faith that moves mountains and makes all the promises of our Lover become a manifested reality.

On the Love Tip: Second

If you're struggling with a dry prayer life or no prayer life at all, if your quiet time with God is not something you look forward to, here's my suggestion. Make a date to meet with God. Select "mood music," set the atmosphere for romance, even have dinner prepared if you like. Or if you're the type who loves to walk and talk, or beautiful scenery is your idea of a nice setting for nurturing intimacy, invite God along and practice being aware of His presence. Ask Him questions about Himself. Don't be the kind of date who says, "Enough of me talking about me. What do *you* think about me?" Earnestly seek to get to know who He is and how He feels about things. Find things in common with His heart. Take your Bible along; it's the longest and best love letter ever written.

When you are in love you want to know everything there is to know about that person. You ask friends, neighbors, and past girlfriends if you can get hold of them. Well, the Bible is the best reference around about the Lover of Your Soul. And instead of just reading the Bible as a reference book or as a how-to guide on Christianity, read it as if you were reading God's private journal. Ask God to guide you to the specific Scriptures that reveal His heart toward you. Begin to journal the things that He shares with you, and then write Him back in the form of a love letter. If people can fall in love over the Internet, falling in love with God should be a cinch! His correspondence can be trusted. Remember, God is not a pushy suitor. Though He longs for you to love Him with all your heart, with all your soul, with all your mind, and with all your strength, He will only take as much as you give, so purpose to give Him your all.

Love Note

Call out to me and I will answer you and tell you great and unsearchable things you do not know.

3

Taking Faith
to Heart

on't worry; he'll be here any minute," Shirley said, not looking the least bit perturbed. I gaped at her in awe. Truly, this was a new Shirley! Gone was Miss Impatient who would shoot you the look of death if you were ten minutes late. (This I had learned through painful experience.) Instead there she sat waiting for HIM, who was an hour and a half tardy. I considered using this instance as blackmail for the next time she gave *me* grief about being late. "Are you sure he's still coming?" I asked in my most nonchalant voice. To be honest, if he had been my date his name would have been crossed out of all my address journals and I would be in my pajamas by now. I couldn't imagine how Shirley could sit there calmly waiting without even glancing at the clock. "But he hasn't even called!" I reminded her. "Oh, something must have come up," she said, still unruffled. "He's usually very punctual."

I didn't know if I should stay or go. Perhaps it would be easier for her to come out of denial and acknowledge that she had been stood up if I left. So I slowly gathered my belongings while surreptitiously sneaking a peek at her to see if she was beginning to crumble. After all, she was so totally into this man. I didn't know if she could bear the disappointment of having HIM let her down. Just as I mumbled something about having to get up early the next morning, the doorbell rang. And Shirley, gliding serenely past me, threw confidently over her shoulder, "See, I told you he would be here. I trust HIM totally!" I slithered past as he was apologetically explaining to Shirley about the pileup he had narrowly missed. He told her about the slowness of the police to restore order and movement to the freeway, and the horror of discovering he had left his cell phone at the office. Amid Shirley's clucking sounds of understanding, I decided I really needed to pray about my jaded nature. Oh, *now* I believed he was telling the truth. But why I was suspicious in the first place was the bigger question.

I had always walked according to the old adage "Believe none of what you hear and half of what you see"—until the purported notion proved to be a concrete fact when it came to people making promises. And so had Shirley until now. But being in love with HIM had changed everything for her. This really started the wheels in my mind turning on the whole issue of trust and faith. Based on the sappy display I had just witnessed, I concluded that what really serves as the foundation for our faith in God's promises is love!

And the Lord *direct your hearts into the* love *of God, and into the patient waiting for Christ.*
—2 Thessalonians 3:5 KJV, emphasis mine

Love surpasses faith. Love waits. Love believes when the mind stops working. Love keeps on believing when the flesh grows weary and fails. Love overcomes all rationale and scientific discussion, all former disappointments, questions, or assumptions. Love looks past all that and simply says, "I believe." The end—by the heart.

Though the fig tree should not blossom,
And there be no fruit on the vines,
Though the yield of the olive should fail,
And the fields produce no food,
Though the flock should be cut off from the fold,
And there be no cattle in the stalls,
Yet I will exult in the LORD, *I will rejoice in the God*
of my salvation.

—Habakkuk 3:17 NASB

Small wonder so many of us struggle with our faith. If God takes too long to do something, we are finished. We pack up the joy of our salvation and swear that He has forsaken us. And our reaction has got to hurt His feelings. Imagine how you'd feel if you had planned to do something nice for someone and, because it took you longer than he felt was an appropriate amount of time, he decided that you were a liar and made other plans instead. Or perhaps he simply thumbed his nose at you and moved on. It's kind of painful when someone disses you because you didn't deliver according to his criteria. Makes you kinda wanna say, "Hey, who am I? Santa Claus?" But God doesn't do that; He keeps on working on the promise in spite of you, timing the appearance of it for when you finally get over yourself and your own designs.

When Moses went up on the mountain to receive the law for the Israelites and stayed away forty days, the Israelites became impatient. Aaron, Moses' brother who had been left in charge, also got caught up in their bad attitudes and assisted the children of Israel in building an idol to worship. Meanwhile Moses was up on the mountaintop with God giving him all of these intricate details concerning Aaron and the priesthood, down to what Aaron should wear as he ministered before Him. He was giving Moses plans for the children of Israel, the commandments, great and wonderful promises of deliverance, provision, and dominion. And they were down below just clowning around because they had no idea about the things God had planned for them. Can you imagine Aaron's embarrassment when he found out? Or the children of Israel's chagrin when Moses came back down and filled them in on all the things God had to say regarding them? All they could do was look silly as they recalled how quickly they had exchanged God for something they could readily see. Their love for God was not at the level where they could just trust, obey, and wait. So many times isn't that us, through and through?

I have been involved with the Weigh Down Diet Workshop for the past several months and it has been an eye-opener for me. At one point in the program I reached a plateau in my weight loss. Every time I got on the scale it seemed as if I had gone up a pound instead of down. In fact, I bounced between the same two pounds for practically a month. It started to affect my psyche. I found myself rationalizing that I could just as well eat what I wanted to because I wasn't losing weight anyway. Finally I caught myself. *Wait a minute!* I had to remind myself. *This whole thing is not about you mechanically losing weight according to a formula. It is about you giving your body back to God as an act of love and obedience.* The premise of the workshop was that by honoring God first above the craving for food, which can be like an idol in our lives, the weight will fall off. So I covenanted with myself not to get back on the scale for two weeks, to simply continue on in obedience out of my love for the Lord with no other motive. Well, wouldn't you know that when I got back on that scale two weeks later, I had lost five pounds! When our faith reaches a plateau, it is love that will keep us healthy and strong in our walk.

Remember the parable of the ten virgins in the twenty-fifth chapter of Matthew? Half of them hadn't anticipated having to wait for the bridegroom, so they only came halfway prepared for the journey to the wedding feast. This later caused them to miss out on the festivities. Sometimes we go to God in prayer about a specific request having already decided when He should answer. We give Him a deadline without knowing all that has to be engineered to deliver what we've asked for. The other thing that gets us into trouble is wondering if our prayer request is just our good idea or a "God idea." Does God agree with what we're asking for? Or is it just a personal whim? If the matter isn't settled, the struggle with our faith is justifiable. But then we have instances when God gives us a specific promise and then nothing happens, so we freak out. This is where the love test comes in to play.

And you shall remember all the way which the LORD your God has led you in the wilderness these forty years, that He might humble you, testing you, to know what was in your heart, whether you would keep His commandments or not.

—Deuteronomy 8:2 NASB, emphasis mine

Sometimes the wait that we endure is not evidence of God's absence. Rather, it indicates the closeness of God searching our hearts and waiting for us to see ourselves as we truly are. Will we take the gift He presents to us and run with it? Or will we still follow after the Giver more than the gift? Would you love Him any less if He never gave you what you asked for? That is the real question. How would you feel if your children only loved you because you gave in to their every whim? How would you feel if you knew they only cared to be with you because of what you could give them? How would you feel if they constantly threw temper tantrums and then stomped off, giving you the silent treatment when they didn't get their way? I think we call those types of children spoiled brats. True love doesn't seek its own way. Its hands are constantly open to the good of everyone involved. It seeks to *please* more than to *be pleased*.

What Kind of Love Is This?

But perhaps we first need to be clear on the matter of love. What is the difference between loving someone and being *in love* with someone? Just loving is an agape thing, that unconditional decision that we make to love someone "with the love of the Lord." Ah, but when you're *in love…* *everything* in you is involved. This is why God asks us to love Him with all our heart, all our mind, all our soul, and all our strength. Though being *in love* might be compared to the eros experience, love born out of intimacy, I would dare to say, it is a combination of agape, eros, and phileo, that brotherly feeling based on fair exchange. In his book *Mere Christianity*, C.S. Lewis called being "in love" love in the second sense. He said that love is not merely a feeling. It is a deep unity, maintained by the will and deliberately strengthened by habit, reinforced (in Christian marriages) by the grace which both partners ask for and receive from God. He went on to say that being "in love" first moves two people to promise fidelity, but it is the quieter agape "I love you in spite of yourself—all that you say and do" love that enabled those same two people to keep the promise. It is agape love that keeps the engine of marriage running, but being "in love" is the explosion that started it.

So what does all of this have to do with having a deep love affair with God? One must understand that loving someone doesn't necessarily mean that every day is filled with tingly sensations. And those days when you feel next to nothing only mean that you're just having one of those days. Love is like the tide of the ocean. It rises and falls in intensity, but the water remains. It's just waiting for the next movement, the next pull on its current from the elements that surround it. Normally we move from coming to God out of fear of judgment or the consequences of our overwhelming circumstances to settling into having faith in Him based on what we are taught about Him and having confirming experiences. But our goal should always be to reach the next level of believing in Him purely out of love.

The fear that leads us to seek protection from God's judgment is good, but we don't want stay there because, left unchecked, fear is accompanied by torment. Fear brings threats of condemnation and perpetual judgment. We must move on to faith because God rightfully earns our trust by the truth of His Word and the confirming "that does it" from His Spirit which dwells within us, a Spirit that is backed up by Him making His promises real to us in innumerable ways. When we press past our minds to get to the heart of it with God, we triumph in the area of faith.

Love...bears all things, believes all things, hopes all things, endures all things. Love never fails....
—1 Corinthians 13:4-8 NASB

And this brings us back full circle to the question of how to get there. There, meaning past fear, past faith, to pure, unadulterated love of God. All I have to offer is one word—intimacy. It was this experience of deep fellowship that caused Abraham to believe God enough to strike out for a land he knew nothing about. As Abraham continued to fellowship with God, God made further promises to Abraham and enlarged the vision of what He wanted to do in Abraham's life. Abraham witnessed the presence of God firsthand as the spirit of the Lord made covenant with Him, passing through the sacrifice of animals that he had prepared. God made Himself visible through a flaming torch and a smoking oven, signifying His ability to lead and preserve Abraham and the descendants that he and Sarai would bear. Intimate fellowship inspired the unconditional faith in the heart of Abraham that caused God to decree him righteous. And Abraham's friendship with God gave him the strength to put his faith into action in order to conceive the child of promise with Sarah.

When someone we love tells us we can do something, we believe him or her. Our knowledge of that person's love for us assures us that he or she would not deceive us. But when we are not secure in the knowledge of that love for us, we tend to waver. What the person is saying might sound good—it might even answer our deepest desire— but without the assurance of where his or her heart is regarding us, we might wonder if we aren't being led down the path to disappointment.

From a Distance

This is what happened to the children of Israel when they balked at the prospect of going into the promised land. Knowing the background of this story is important in order to understand what happened here. The Lord decided to come down to visit the children of Israel because He wanted them to hear His voice. He also wanted them to witness that He spoke to Moses in order for them to respect his leadership. So on the appointed day of visitation, the Lord came down and the people freaked out. They decided they were afraid of God and magnanimously gave Moses the charge to go talk with Him, then come back and tell them what this frightening God had said. This was the first company of lazy Christians. "All right, pastor, you fellowship with God and then come tell us what He said on Sunday morning. We have no desire to meet with Him ourselves." Hmm...I knew you could relate!

But something deep happened when the children of Israel made this shortsighted decision. When they forfeited the presence of God in their lives, they forfeited their opportunity for intimacy with Him, for personal exchange. Now they were merely receiving secondhand conversation. Think about it. Moses could have come back and told them anything, such as, "God said give me all your money." We know of the blatant misuse of the terms "pastor" and "man of God" these days. The horror stories around us abound as charlatans in the church lead many astray. We've opened ourselves up to this type of deception because of our own lack of participation in relationship with God and our inadequate knowledge of His Word. It was always God's intention for His people to fellowship with Him individually, yet most flee from the opportunity. Let's face it; to go into the presence of God takes courage. It takes courage because it makes you face who you really are, and most of us are not ready to watch that movie.

So here are all these Israelites watching Moses going into the Tent of Meetings to commune with God. The Bible says that they stood in the doorways of their own tents and watched him go in. They worshipped God from where they stood, never pressing in any closer to meet with Him. This was not laying a firm foundation for trusting God for things to come. There was a major disconnect here. Knowing *about* someone and *knowing* someone are two completely different things. The first is a surface experience that will only stand firm if it isn't tried. But *knowing* someone and being involved with that person intimately lays the foundation for standing the tests of time, wear, and difficulty. This is why employers check references. Your resume is one thing, but the experience your past coworkers have had with you lets a potential employer know if you are a person who can be trusted. Qualifications aside, it is really the heart of the person that an employer seeks to know.

Well, the Israelites had all of God's qualifications down pat. He could feed them when they were hungry. He could kill their enemies. He could do this and that, but *would He?* Why, after experiencing His provision, would this still be the question in their minds during every new challenge? The answer to that question is simple. They didn't know the heart of God.

...But the people who know their God will display strength and take action.
—Daniel 11:32 NASB

They didn't know His heart because they had forfeited their own personal access to Him. Without intimacy, His heart would remain a mystery to them. They would never know how much He longed for them to experience the fullness of all His promises. So now here they stood on the brink of going into the promised land, balking. They couldn't see it. How did they know that God would protect them from the giants in the land? They couldn't be sure. They didn't know His heart.

In all the great company of Israel, only three people could embrace the vision—Moses, Joshua, and Caleb. What separated these three men from the rest of the Israelites? One thing—their relationship with God. These were three who didn't stand afar off. Instead, they entered into relationship with God. We already know about Moses. Joshua had gone up the mountain with Moses. He had remained in the tabernacle in the presence of God even after Moses left. And God vouched for Caleb by telling Moses that Caleb had a "different spirit" and had followed Him wholeheartedly all his life. These three men had pressed past the surface, had pressed past receiving a word from someone else concerning God, and had entered in to see God for themselves. In their relationship with God they had come to love Him as well as acknowledge and serve Him. This is the only way they could follow God wholeheartedly. They had no doubt that God would do what He said. But those who had chosen to stand on the fringes of their relationship with Him had nothing to go on, so they stalled and broke down before even coming close to crossing the finish line.

This made God mad. So mad, in fact, that He wanted to wipe out all of the Israelites and start from scratch, but Moses pleaded their case and asked God to give them a break. And God responded that He would do as Moses had

asked specifically because they had established a friendship. God called Moses His friend! Do you know that when
you get to the place where you have a real friendship with
God, there will be times you can persuade Him to extend
His grace to give another person a chance to come into a
right standing with God? God's initial judgment was hell
and damnation for us until Jesus interceded and paid the
price. Based on His relationship with the Son, God
embraces us into His heavenly family. So because Moses
was a friend to God, he was able to stay God's hand from
striking the children of Israel for their lack of faith. When
we are friends with God, in a deep and abiding relationship with Him, we, too, can ask for favors on the behalf of
others in accordance with His will. Again, it is all about
relationship. This is the call of an intercessor to serve as a
bridge between the needs of those here on earth and the
hand of God.

*I ask on their behalf; I do not ask on behalf of the
world, but of those whom Thou hast given Me; for
they are Thine; and all things that are Mine are
Thine, and Thine are Mine; and I have been glorified
in them.*

—John 17:9 NASB

Jesus counted on His relationship with the Father being
enough of a deposit against the return of our love back to
God. He was willing to bet on it with His life. He was intimate with the Father. They had the ultimate love relationship. Their hearts were transparent toward one another.
They trusted one another. They had faith in one another's
intentions. Where the holiness of God created a gap He

could not cross to connect to man, Jesus filled the space in between with mutual love. And even now, as Jesus sits at the right hand of the Father interceding on our behalf, God's hand is stayed from judgment and moved to bless us because of the prayers of the One who died for us. God shows up for His friends.

In Love and War

When the Israelites hid quivering from Goliath, the Philistine giant, a little shepherd boy stepped up to save the day. He did it without any armor or sophisticated weaponry. This is the one God called a man after His own heart. David, who has been called the romantic warrior, didn't give a second thought to challenging the giant who dared to defy the armies of the living God. How dare Goliath, this overgrown excuse for a man, insult his God like that? Kind of reminds me of the sixties tune "Don't Mess with Bill." The girl was saying she loved her man; therefore, no-one had better mess with him! That's how David felt. Nobody was going to talk about the Lover of His Soul with such contempt and get away with it! Why, he knew God intimately. He sang to Him and worshipped Him in the fields and pastures. They communed together, he and God. When he was in danger, God backed him up and helped him slay the lion and the bear that came against him. So this giant was no biggie (pardon the pun). When Saul tried to give David something else to trust in—namely, his armor—David said he couldn't use it because he hadn't tested it. He couldn't vouch for the armor's reputation. He wasn't familiar or comfortable with it. He would go out with only the one thing he could trust—his God.

Without so much as flinching in the presence of the giant, David told Goliath to get ready to bow to the God of Israel. He wanted all who were looking to take note that the Living God was not to be taken lightly. So take that! And he finished Goliath off with the first of a handful of rocks, then went on his way. And here we sit, worrying about the mundane. Will God bless me with this or bless me with that? When was the last day *you* faced a hostile giant?

I don't mean to downplay your present situation, but, as David said, "If God could show up for that other stuff, surely He will show up for this." Amen! Shout the victory. If you can't, you need to adjust your love meter. Love not only covers a multitude of sins, it has the ability to believe in the impossible.

On the Love Tip: Third

If you're struggling with your faith, do like David did and rehearse the previous times when God has delivered His promises and taken your defense in troubled situations. Sometimes, when faced with new tribulations, we develop amnesia about past victories. But God has not changed personalities. He remains faithful as always. So ask God to increase your love for Him. He knows best how to get to your heart. Keep a journal and begin composing your own psalms to Him like David, who wrote everything down. He recorded everything—what others were doing to him, how he felt about his enemies. But here is the most important hint of all. Here is the secret love builder. After David finished venting about the reality of his problems—a practice that flies in the face of present-day faith teachings—he concluded with a "but God" statement. For instance, "God, my enemies have come upon me to eat up my flesh, but I know You will show up and they will stumble and fall."

Think about how you feel when someone comes to your defense. It warms your heart toward that person, doesn't it? Well, God gets furious when the enemy attacks your life. He grieves over your lack and your losses. Psalm 56:8 says that He takes account of all of our wanderings, that He collects all of our tears in a bottle and records them in His book. It's so wonderful that I almost can't stand it. God writes down in His book, "On such and such day, so and so made Michelle cry." He loves us that much! Now, how can you not love a God like that?

ℒ*ove* 𝒩*ote*

I am the one who will go with you; I will never fail you or forsake you. I will continually surround you with my lovingkindness.

4

Romancing the Stone

*S*hirley hunched over the wheel of the sports car that belonged to HIM, concentrating intensely on weaving her way through the traffic that inched along at a snail's pace in the rush hour congestion. "Why don't you just get on the freeway?" I asked. "Oh, no," she answered. "He would have a fit. He has this thing about taking this car on the freeway during peak traffic time." I responded, "But he isn't here! He'll never know!" Shirley shot me a horrified look, as if I had suggested that we rob a bank. "How could you propose such a thing?" she said. "It's not about whether he would know or not. I would never do something behind his back that he didn't approve of!" I couldn't believe my ears. Shirley was the queen of the "what they don't know won't hurt them" philosophy. The girl had to be gone.

Anyone would understand how I was feeling if they were sitting in this traffic. From my window I could see the cars on the freeway zipping along freely as we sat there watching a construction worker feebly attempt to move us around the island that had been set up in the middle of the road. Our lane looked like an endless parking lot. As the radio blasted "If Loving You Is Wrong, I Don't Wanna Be Right," I just looked at Shirley singing along at the top of her lungs and shook my head. Truly, in her case, loving HIM was right and she didn't want to do anything wrong. This love thing sure was deep.

To reflect back on my own love life, I have fond remembrances of dating a man from France who requested that I learn French so I could converse with his friends. 'Nuff said. Off to French class I went and, though the relationship fell by the wayside, to this day I still "parlez francais" very well, thank you. Speaking of words, I recall my reaction to a Christian friend of mine whose conversation was peppered with profanity during stressful times. "Good gravy!" I exploded. "I have learned an entire language to make the man I love happy. If you love the Lord one tiny morsel, couldn't you drop a few ugly words from your vocabulary? It's got to be easier than what I've been through!" So how much should we love God? And how do we show that love? Good question. Jesus said it pretty succinctly.

If you love Me, you will keep My commandments.
—John 14:15 NASB

Ouch! I thought for the longest time that I was simply supposed to be obedient because God said so. You know, religious duty performed by rote. I never equated my obedience as a sign of my love for Him. That was a real revelation to me, and it changed my attitude as well as my actions. I had to admit that some of my obedience had nothing to do with God. I feared the consequences of my actions more than I feared God. On the other hand, I was sometimes disobedient in instances where I thought I wouldn't be caught. Sad, but true. Being obedient because I loved God and didn't want to hurt His heart was the last thing on my mind. I had forgotten that He was watching my disobedience, whether other people saw me or not. I had not considered how my disobedience even in the small things grieved His heart. I forgot that He took my behavior as His child quite personally.

For this is the love of God, that we keep His commandments; and His commandments are not burdensome.

—1 John 5:3 NASB

I imagine in my mind's eye God saying, "Gee, Michelle, if you really loved Me, you wouldn't mind doing what I ask of you. Why is it such a hardship to be obedient to Me? I haven't asked you to match the sacrifice I made for you. The things I ask of you are for your own sake and your own blessing, yet you give Me such a hard time." Think about it, why don'tcha?

Loving 'Til It Hurts

Perhaps the root of our problem is that we *don't* truly see the sacrifice that Jesus made for us. I think the mantra, "Christ died, Christ rose, Christ will come again," has been repeated so many times that it has become a passé ideology to many. It doesn't mean what it should mean. We see photos and statues of Jesus looking like an exhausted ballet dancer, so exquisitely graceful in His suffering that we fail to grasp the depth of pain that He really endured. Somehow these beautiful renditions of His crucifixion do not convey the horror of what He went through for us. Perhaps we need to switch places with Him for a moment.

Just imagine, here you are living in the splendor of heaven where everything is lovely, clean, glorious, and perfect. Angels are singing your praises and worshipping you as if you were the best thing since sliced bread. But some events going on down on the earth distract you. You're a compassionate type, so you decide to help out the lost souls who need you. And you plummet to the earth where you experience the greatest culture shock of all. The same people you came to save are, for the most part, hostile toward you. In fact, they blatantly reject you for no good reason. The main cross section of people who flock to you comes grasping for what they can get for themselves. They're not really interested in you. They come seeking a miracle or looking for an opportunity to trip you up and dismantle your reputation. They simply want to use you. Your closest friends are twelve men who don't get it, but they're nice and they're doing the best they can. One of them, however, is stealing from you and another has a big mouth that threatens to get everybody in trouble. The public is terribly fickle, vacillating on who they want to follow, and why, from day to day. Those who claim to know your Father are all sanctimonious snakes in the grass. You find yourself surrounded by needless confusion. Then, after all your effort at teaching them, your companions flee when the going gets tough. One of your own men even betrays you! You get hauled off to a trial that is a travesty of justice. People are brought in to lie about your character and actions. The same people who sang your praises are now calling for your crucifixion. You've been betrayed.

The Jewish soldiers blindfold you and then take turns hitting you, taunting you to tell them who hit you. They yank entire clumps of your beard out of your face. Then you get beaten within an inch of your life.

Let's stop and talk about this beating for a minute. Jesus was beaten with a cat-o'-nine-tails, a whip composed of leather strips with shreds of glass embedded in it. Every time those leather strips slashed against His skin, they tore away flesh, then muscle, then ligament until the bare bones of His back were exposed. At forty lashes you were declared legally dead; that's why they stopped at thirty-nine. (Though we are not told how many lashes Jesus actually recieved, we can be certain the punishment was brutal.) They wanted the satisfaction of torturing Him even further. The Roman soldiers stripped Him, put a scarlet robe on Him, and crushed a crown of thorns on His head, mocking His royalty. They beat him with a staff. Isaiah prophesied that Jesus was unrecognizable by the time they were finished beating Him, and it was true. Doesn't quite match the pictures we see, does it? Think about the sting of when you stub your toe or smash a finger, then intensify the pain countless times. That's what Jesus endured for you. But it doesn't stop there. Let's return to imagining ourselves in His place.

You endure the beating and, before you can try to draw your next breath, they weigh you down with a heavy cross that you must now drag through town on your way to your own crucifixion. Does this bring back memories of when your mother or father told you to go and get the belt or switch so they could spank you? You thought that was cruel and unusual punishment. Well, that is no comparison to crucifixion! So the people crucify you. They strip you and nail your wrists and feet to the cross, and put you on display in front of your peers. The pain is unbearable. The weight of your body is squeezing the breath out of your lungs. Your bones are threatening to pop out of their joints from the strain of hanging there.

Then they auction off your clothing in front of you as you hang dying. Talk about no respect. Truly, you have seen better days in heaven, yet you say nothing. Jeering and taunting you to call the angels to save you if you're so acquainted with God, they get in their last digs. And you still find it in your heart to say, "Father, forgive them for they know not what they do." Is that picture enough to make you throw out the romantic notions of the crucifixion and deal with the gruesome reality that was the price of your redemption? And all He asks for in return is your love. Think about His love for you, what He did for you, what He would have done for you even if you were the only person on the face of the earth. And some of you haven't spoken to someone for years because that person looked at you the wrong way!

The deepest truth about this whole thing is that Jesus knew what would happen to Him before He came. He knew that He would be rejected, yet He was willing to come anyway. Most of us wouldn't go around the corner for someone who wasn't nice to us. But Jesus, who for the joy that was set before Him, endured the shame, endured the cross—for the sake of you and me. For the few who would come to believe in Him, the pain was worth it. Jesus was willing to die for us even when He knew the worst about us. How many people do you know who you could tell your deepest, darkest secrets to and not worry about that knowledge changing the way they felt about you? Not many, right? Yet Jesus gave His life for that very information and continues to love us fervently, calling us His bride. The best and the worst of us are safe with Him. I don't know any other man capable of that kind of love, do you?

Cleaning House

One day running out of my apartment on my way to an appointment, I cast a glance back through my doorway into the room. The place was a mess. Things thrown everywhere in haste. Complete disorganization. The Lord spoke to me right there and said, "This room reflects your spiritual condition." I was mortified. But it was true. So many times we fail to realize that our surrounding circumstances and outward behavior reflect what our heart looks like to God.

Behold, I stand at the door and knock; if anyone hears My voice and opens the door, I will come in to him and will dine with him, and he with Me.
—Revelation 3:20 NASB

Have you ever thought of Jesus as a dinner date? We invite Him into our hearts, but we are not willing to clean up so that He can be comfortable and joyful in His new abode. If you can, just picture God stepping over dirty underwear, spoiled food, and various kinds of garbage in your heart. Why would He want to stay in a pig's sty when heaven is so beautiful? Yet He does want to live in your heart. What's more, He is even willing to help you clean it up! He wants to make a love nest in your soul. Single women, He is the only man you get to live with before marriage!

Just as the Father has loved Me, I have also loved you; abide in My love.
—John 15:9 NASB, emphasis mine

If we really love Him, we will do everything in our power to make Him feel at home. Jesus is the perfect room-mate because He doesn't mind sharing the household chores with you. It's all right to ask Him to help you move some things out of the way. He delights in showing Himself strong for you. He is thrilled to take the garbage out, but He waits for you to ask.

Setting the Atmosphere

When we know that a prospective beau or significant other is coming to visit us, what do we do? We clean up! First we scour the house from top to bottom. Then we take a bath, brush our teeth, and put on perfume and nice clothes. We spray the room with air freshener, light candles, we do whatever little individual touches it takes to impress this man. I know you're with me here. I've done it and you've done it. We go through all of this for a mortal man who is limited in his ability to love us, while the true Lover of Our Soul gets the leftovers of our hearts. I get this picture of God watching us go through all these gyrations and saying to Himself, "Funny, she doesn't go through all those changes for Me. She comes to Me looking any old kind of way. She doesn't care what I stumble over or sit down on in her heart. She doesn't care what her thoughts smell like to me." Ewww! Go ahead, take a deep breath. Never thought about it that way, did you? But now you know you need to try to look pretty on the inside for the One who loves you most. Purity is His favorite color. Sanctification is His favorite scent, and He really feels comfortable sitting in chairs that are upholstered with holiness. So that's why He says that all the law hangs on the first two love command-ments. Jesus knows that when we really love someone, our actions speak louder than our words.

When we're in love, we will change the color of our hair, the type of clothes we wear, anything to please the object of our affection. And so it should be with our relationship with God. Do you know that if we truly loved the Lord, we wouldn't even have to check the list of "do not's"? We would anticipate His heart and act accordingly. When we truly love someone, we won't worship other things before that person. We won't lie, steal, cheat, kill, or covet their personal things because we are too busy protecting their best interest. We wouldn't allow anyone else to think or speak badly of our loved ones, whether they be God or a human being. Because when we truly love as God told us to, with all our heart, soul, mind, and strength, we love the other person the way we love ourselves. And that's as good as it gets because we take very good care of ourselves. We pamper ourselves, protecting ourselves from pain and injury, feeding and clothing our bodies, and making sure that we keep ourselves clean. Why? Because, beyond securing our own state of well-being, our reputation is at stake if we don't put our best foot forward. What would people think of us? If love for God is not the motivating factor in our behavior and state of heart, we affect His reputation. What do people say whenever we mess up? "I thought she was a Christian!" Do you really want your Lover's name disgraced because of your actions?

David understood that he needed to get his act together because the name of the Lord would be affected if he didn't. He loved God enough to be truly repentant when caught in sin because his first thought was how God felt about it. He mourned over grieving God's heart, more than he regretted the consequences he was sentenced to bear or the injury done to his own household. It caused him to cry, "I have sinned against the Lord" (2 Samuel 12:13). This made God cherish David even more.

Joseph, when faced with the temptation of Potiphar's wife, didn't first ponder the consequences of getting caught. His reaction to her sinful suggestion was, "How can I do this awful thing against God? How would God feel if I committed adultery with you?" While many in his position would have justified falling headfirst into this dalliance, Joseph stood firm. He could have decided, "What the heck? God has forsaken me anyway. My brothers sold me into slavery unjustly, and God did nothing to intervene. Why should I care what He thinks? Obviously, He didn't think enough of me in the first place to save me from my predicament. I'm unhappy in my situation. Potiphar's wife is unhappy in her marriage. Comforting one another would be perfectly justified." No! Joseph didn't go there. No matter how many human arguments could have supported his fall from grace, all he knew was that he would hurt the heart of God if he partook of these stolen waters. And for whatever it was worth, no matter what God hadn't done for him yet, he preferred to take his chances with God and remain holy. God rewarded Joseph in the end and he gave the glory to the Lord who brought him out, finally seeing His plan all along and deeming it a wise and good thing.

The Hebrew boys, when faced with the choice between bowing before the golden image that Nebuchadnezzar had erected or being thrown into the fiery furnace, were willing to go for broke rather than offend God. Their answer threw old Nebby into a fit of rage. The nerve of those Hebrew upstarts! He couldn't believe his ears.

Shadrach, Meshach and Abed-nego answered and said to the king, "O Nebuchadnezzar, we do not need to give you an answer concerning this matter. If it be so, our God whom we serve is able to deliver us from

the furnace of blazing fire; and He will deliver us out
of your hand, O king. But even if He does not, let it
be known to you, O king, that we are not going to
serve your gods or worship the golden image that you
have set up.

—Daniel 3:16-18 NASB

Only passion about the God you serve could make you stand in the face of a death threat like that. To say that you don't care if God rescues you or not, that you still will not forsake Him is some sho-nuff love! Think about the saints mentioned in the book of Revelation who overcame the enemy by the blood of the Lamb and the word of their testimony and did not love their life, even when faced with death (Revelation 12:11). Why? Because they loved Someone more than their own lives! They loved the Lord. Perhaps that's why He also asked us to love Him with all of our strength. In some cases that's exactly what it takes to hold on to living the sanctified life. We are told we cannot serve two masters because we will love one and despise the other (Luke 16:13). This is why Paul advises singles to celebrate their singleness, citing the fact that once they got married, their devotion to God would be divided. So many things pull at us—the lust of the flesh, the lust of the eyes, all the things that contribute to the pride of life. It is a struggle to remain single-minded, single-hearted, when it comes to God. He does not deserve the fickleness of our hearts. It's up to us to take dominion of our own will and purpose to nurture our love for our Lord.

Think about it in these terms. If a king was coming to your house for dinner, would you serve him leftovers? Yet this is what many of us do with God. Everything else comes first—especially our flesh. We seem to have a rationalization for every single one of our weaknesses.

I remember my chagrin at my first Weigh Down Workshop when I was hit with the news that my overeating was disobedience to God. I felt a wave of despair wash over me. I had given God my cigarettes, my unedifying music collection. I had even given Him my body and was living a celibate lifestyle. Couldn't He at least allow me to fill the gap with food? It was the one thing that didn't involve anyone else besides myself. How could anything that seemed so good be sin? But I was reminded that my body was the temple of the Holy Spirit, and He didn't want to be squashed to death in His dwelling place by my fat! Although to be fair, He did give my soul permission to delight itself in another kind of fatness (Isaiah 55:2). I was relieved to know I could be fat somewhere. But that didn't solve the dilemma of my love for food.

Oh, mercy me! I thought. Will the list of things that I must surrender to God never end? Then I stopped and thought about how much the Lord had blessed me, and I was embarrassed by my thoughts. How could I love food more than God? That was absolutely ridiculous. The food was killing me! It was slowing me down, upsetting my system, robbing me of wearing beautiful clothes, and hurting my feet. How could I cling to something that was so cruel to me? My obsession with food was like having a bad man in my life. When I chose to release yet another portion of my heart to God, food lost its importance and its power over me. Oh, every now and then my tastebuds behave like an old lover trying to lure me back to the fold of overindulging my flesh, but I've determined that I love God more. As the weight fell off and I began to rediscover things in my closet that I hadn't worn in years, I knew that

I really loved God more! Truly, He is a lover who puts the joy back in loving and gives good gifts.

As I remembered my car trip with Shirley and experienced a moment of conviction for urging her to do something that wouldn't be pleasing to HIM, I had to stop and give my friend kudos for not being swayed by my impatience. It was clear to me that she was reaping the benefits of being obedient to HIM and honoring his wishes. I mean, here we were luxuriating in his expensive foreign sports car! Shirley had proven she could be trusted with all that belonged to HIM. Though love was the motivating factor for her doing what he asked of her, in the end she gained more than it cost her. She had received definite benefits that could be seen with the naked eye. He was continually giving her expensive gifts in addition to allowing her access to all of his possessions. As we choose to obey God out of a pure heart filled with love for Him, we prove to Him that we can be trusted with rich blessings also.

The gift of salvation is free, and yes, God gives us a plethora of blessings simply out of His marvelous grace. But then there is this burgeoning chest of blessings that are conditional. We receive these blessings only in response to our obedience to Him. He leaves the choice up to us. Every day we get to select life or death, blessings or curses, for our lives.

I call heaven and earth to record this day against you, that I have set before you life and death, blessing and cursing: therefore choose life, that both thou and thy seed may live.

—Deuteronomy 30:19 KJV, emphasis mine

What does that mean, Michelle? you might ask. It means that there's more to this life than being born again or saved or whatever your denomination calls it. There is the fullness of life that God wants every believer to experience. However, He needs our cooperation in order for us to experience life the way He originally designed it to be experienced. Because Adam walked and talked in faultless fellowship with God and was completely obedient, he received the fullness of God's blessing. He lived in complete righteousness, peace, and joy—the description of the Kingdom of God. Think about it. There was no stress or strain involved in living. The animals around Adam lived in peace. There was no crime, no lack, no disease. He had direct access to God. They walked and talked together in the cool of the evening, side by side in the garden. The earth watered itself, and abundant vegetation yielded itself voluntarily to Adam's disposal. Everything literally existed in anticipation of Adam's needs. Even God anticipated Adam's needs and supplied him with them before Adam even needed to ask. For instance, Adam didn't even have to ask God for a mate. God just decided he needed one and made him his perfect match! Now how do you like that?

Anyway, we all know that Adam and Eve messed up that perfect arrangement for the rest of us. I should state here that the line forms behind me when we get to heaven. I want to be the first to fuss at them! (Actually, they will probably be the last thing on my mind when I am finally in the presence of the Lover of My Soul.) To move right along, God made a way for us to get back to the state of Kingdom living by suggesting that we make sound decisions when faced with the temptation to press past His instructions. It's nothing deep. Plain and simple, it's totally up to us. All we have to do is choose to be obedient.

*And it shall come to pass, if thou shalt hearken dili-
gently unto the voice of the* LORD *thy God, to observe
and to do all his commandments which I command
thee this day, that the* LORD *thy God will set thee on
high above all nations of the earth: And all these blessings shall come on thee, and overtake thee, if thou
shalt hearken unto the voice of the* LORD *thy God.
Blessed shalt thou be in the city, and blessed shalt
thou be in the field. Blessed shall be the fruit of thy
body, and the fruit of thy ground, and the fruit of thy
cattle, the increase of thy kine, and the flocks of thy
sheep. Blessed shall be thy basket and thy store.
Blessed shalt thou be when thou comest in, and
blessed shalt thou be when thou goest out. The* LORD
*shall cause thine enemies that rise up against thee to
be smitten before thy face: they shall come out against
thee one way, and flee before thee seven ways. The*
LORD *shall command the blessing upon thee in thy
storehouses, and in all that thou settest thine hand
unto; and he shall bless thee in the land which the*
LORD *thy God giveth thee....And all people of the
earth shall see that thou art called by the name of the*
LORD; *and they shall be afraid of thee. And the* LORD
*shall make thee plenteous in goods, in the fruit of thy
body...The* LORD *shall open unto thee his good treasure, the heaven to give the rain unto thy land in his
season, and to bless all the work of thine hand: and
thou shalt lend unto many nations, and thou shalt
not borrow. And the* LORD *shall make thee the head,
and not the tail; and thou shalt be above only, and
thou shalt not be beneath; if that thou hearken unto
the commandments of the* LORD *thy God, which I*

command thee this day, to observe and to do them:
And thou shalt not go aside from any of the words
which I command thee this day, to the right hand, or
to the left, to go after other gods to serve them. But it
shall come to pass, if thou wilt not hearken unto the
voice of the LORD thy God, to observe to do all his
commandments and his statutes which I command
thee this day; that all these curses shall come upon
thee, and overtake thee.

—Deuteronomy 28:1-15 KJV

You can read about the curses for yourself. The bottom line is this: The next time someone asks you how a loving God can send people to hell, your reply should be, "He doesn't. People choose their own destiny." God has given us free will, but He has also educated us on all of our options. To bless someone who is disobedient would be like giving an infant the keys to a Porsche. The baby would crash the car and hurt himself. An infant would not be able to handle all that power. He wouldn't know how to steer it, wouldn't even come close to being able to see over the steering wheel. So God is not going to give you anything He knows you can't handle. It would be cruel of Him to give you things to your own detriment. Instead, He teaches us from His Word and releases us to choose. He then rewards us according to our actions and attitudes. This is why it is important to be *cheerful* and motivated by love in our obedience. We curse our own lives if we choose to walk in grudging obedience. This mode of life, religious and legalistic, brings curses. No one is inspired to bless a sourpuss even if she is doing the right thing. Her attitude takes all the joy out of it.

Because thou servedst not the LORD thy God with joyfulness, and with gladness of heart, for the abundance of all things; Therefore shalt thou serve thine enemies which the LORD shall send against thee, in hunger, and in thirst, and in nakedness, and in want of all things: and he shall put a yoke of iron upon thy neck, until he have destroyed thee.
—Deuteronomy 28:47,48 KJV

Here is where the love part comes in. Loving Him even when we fail buys us extra grace. Because He is so loving, sometimes He gives us blessings of encouragement if our heart is turned toward Him. Isn't that sweet? He gently urges us toward the finish line of obedience. And once we achieve the victory, the trophies on the other side are doozies! You read the list above—prosperity, fruitfulness, victory over our enemies, a lasting inheritance. You name it, He pulls out all the stops! So, needless to say, there is a chain reaction thing going on here. The more we love Him, the more obedient we will be. The more obedient we are, the more He blesses us. He'll allow us to drive His flashy car (like my friend Shirley), handle His money, own His property, have access to all He has. Why? Because He can trust us to do the right thing with them! Because He knows that if our hearts are linked to His, our passions are the same. We will like what He likes and hate what He hates. Wow! It doesn't get any simpler than that, does it?

When we truly love God, what is important to Him will also become important to us. We will like what He likes and dislike what He dislikes. "But whoever keeps His word, truly the love of God is perfected in him" (see 1 John 2:5). This is why Jesus prayed, "Thy kingdom come, Thy will be done." He loved the Father and wanted what the Father wanted. He was totally surrendered to the Father's heart. He, too, learned obedience by the things He suffered for the sake of the Father's pleasure (Hebrews 5:8). Sometimes obedience will stretch us beyond our personal pleasure level. Sometimes it will be downright uncomfortable. But for the sake of love you will lay aside your desires and turn your back on disobedience, being willing to give Him your very life. Because that's what love does.

On the Love Tip: Fourth

If you're struggling in the area of obedience, sit down and record your weaknesses on a sheet of paper. Write down why you desire these things. Now jot down how God feels about each one of these desires and why. You will find that the reason He dislikes those things is because they are harmful to you. God is jealous but not selfish. He jealously guards our hearts and wants to keep them for Himself because He knows that He alone can fill our empty souls. A full soul can pass by the greatest of temptations because it is already satisfied. Ask God to give you a specific word to increase your love for Him. Make a date with Him for dinner. Set the atmosphere with worship music and purpose to begin practicing intimacy with Him the way you would with the man in your life. When you sit down to visit with Him, tell Him all of the reasons why He is wonderful. You'll find that you can get on quite a roll as the Holy Spirit begins to bring things to your remembrance. Ask Him to give you a heart of flesh that is tender toward Him. Ask Him to make the reality of His sacrifice for you come alive in your heart. Bask in His presence as He begins to pour Himself out on you, and feel the love grow.

Love Note

Because I love you, I will bless you and keep you. I will make my face to shine upon you and be gracious to you. I cover you with my countenance and give you peace.

5
Through Love-Colored Glasses

Shirley closed her eyes and leaned back against the chair's headrest, directing a make-believe orchestra with one finger artfully suspended in space. I watched her in absolute amazement. Her face was the perfect picture of unadulterated bliss. It was as if she had been transported to another space in time. She was completely oblivious to anything else. She hummed along with the cellos as they battled with the violins. And all I could wonder was, *When did Shirley become so passionate about classical music?* But I dared not interrupt her rapture. As the piece built to a crescendo and her movements became even more pronounced, she abruptly lurched to the edge of her chair and finished conducting with one wild wave of her arms.

Exhausted but seemingly satisfied, she slumped down, looking as if she had just accomplished some Olympian feat and could now relax and rest upon her laurels. "Mmm, wasn't Mozart something else? No wonder Salieri was jealous!" she exclaimed. I shook my head as if trying to clear away the fog of my incredulity. "What? Since when have *you* gotten so into classical music? I thought you hated it," I said pointedly. "Oh, that was before I met HIM," she sighed. "You know, sometimes when you don't understand something, you tend not to like it. But he explains the pieces so well, you can just see them come alive. It's incredible! I mean, couldn't you just feel the passion in that piece?" But I hadn't really heard the music. I was too caught up in watching the transformation of my friend from funk enthusiast to connoisseur of what she had once termed "watered-down sap."

"I'm starving," Shirley breathed, still slightly winded from her musical ecstasy. "Let's get something to eat. Do you like sushi?" "Sushi?" I echoed. "You mean those raw fish things you swore you would never eat? The same sushi you watched me eat as you pretended to gag and ruined my dinner? You mean *that* sushi?" A sheepish grin crept across her face. "Oh, yes. I forgot you liked it. But yours was different." I smiled in amusement. "Shirley, all sushi is basically the same with varying degrees of freshness. So when did we start eating sushi, hmm?" I stressed the *we*, figuring that by this time, she knew that I knew that her changing palate had everything to do with HIM. "Well, you know, each day with HIM is a new experience. I just love it; he has just opened up a whole new world to me! Who would have ever thought that good ole meat-and-potatoes me would be craving sushi?" she confessed. "Yeah, go figure," I mumbled under my breath.

As we got ready to go out, Shirley stopped to pull an overcoat from her hall closet. "Where did you get that?" I shrieked, not realizing my voice had jumped five decibels. So shocked was I at the sight of this loud, red jacket being flung over her shoulders, I jumped back as if someone had leapt out to frighten me from a hidden corner. Shirley *never* wore red! Or any other notable color for that matter. She was the queen of black, white, navy, and gray. She said all other colors should be left in the rainbow where they belonged. "Oh, this was a present from HIM. Isn't it lovely?" she purred, stroking the lapel as if she were smoothing the pelt of a mink coat. "He just loves jewel tones. That reminds me, I have this little emerald green number on hold over at Sak's. He's gonna love it when he sees me in it." I couldn't believe my eyes or my ears. I almost no longer recognized my friend of so many years! In a few months this man had managed to completely renovate her way of thinking. And though none of it seemed to be harmful, Shirley's behavior continued to make me very introspective about my relationship with God. Had my way of thinking changed since knowing Him? Did I love what He loved? Hate what He hated? Could I truly say that my mind was renewed? Or was I picking and choosing which of His opinions were convenient for me to embrace?

Here was Shirley completely revamping major portions of her life based on the tastes of the man in her life, while many who supposedly have a relationship with God continue to live compromised lives simply because they never take the time to see things the way God truly sees them. It's got to be a love issue. It is in the longing to become one with a person that we begin to make adjustments in our own perspectives and priorities. It is in the desire to be closer than close to that person that we desire to see what they see, feel what they feel, taste what they taste, smell what they smell. We literally stretch beyond ourselves to live through the other's senses, so great is our hunger to relate to them on every level. The more we agree on and have in common, the closer we are. The realistic truth is that opposites attract but the closer they get, the more they begin to repel one another. There are not enough similarities between two opposites to create a tight bond that will endure through any type of real pressure. Why? Because opposites will have radically different opinions about how to deal with various situations.

Shirley and her man had a lot of things in common, but the gap was closing in those areas where they differed. I noticed that she enthusiastically inhaled all information concerning HIM. She listened to everything he said and watched HIM intently. She was determined to please HIM in every way. Being a wise woman, she knew that the best way to please a man was to give him what he wanted. Therefore if he loved classical music, she would learn to love it. If he liked red, she would wear plenty of it. If he liked sushi, she would be right there eating it with him. Some of you just got nauseous, I know. But the bottom line in this exercise is that Shirley was getting what she wanted. Her man was filled with adoration for her and constantly showered her with costly gifts. Now it must be noted that Shirley was no pushover. She was a wise woman who carefully chose her battles. For her, winning the war meant keeping her love life intact.

It's a Love Thang

Have you ever noticed that the longer married couples are together, the more they begin to look alike? That is the principle of becoming one. The more we walk together, the more we begin to live inside of one another. Our individual agendas begin to pale in comparison to the beauty of mutual dreams and desires. That is when couples experience the breakthrough of truly enjoying their relationship.

The fight is over. No more trying to bend the other person to your will. No more wishing he would change. No more digging in your heels and fighting to the finish for your own identity and way of doing things. There is a mellowing, a smoothing of the edges where you now rub one another gently, buffing one another to a beautiful glow that reflects your oneness. Couples at this stage can even finish each other's sentences, they know each other so well. God wants this same type of relationship with us. He takes all concerning us very personally. He anticipates our every thought. He feels our every need. We should be able to finish His sentences. How do we do that? By doing what He would do if He were here.

Then the King will say to those on His right, "Come, you who are blessed of My Father, inherit the kingdom prepared for you from the foundation of the world. For I was hungry and you gave Me something to eat; I was thirsty, and you gave Me drink; I was a stranger, and you invited Me in; naked and you clothed Me; I was sick, and you visited Me; I was in prison, and you came to Me." Then the righteous will answer Him, saying, "Lord, when did we see You hungry, and feed You, or thirsty, and give You drink? And when did we see You a stranger, and invite You in, or naked, and clothe You? And when did we see You sick, or in prison, and come to You?" And the King will answer and say to them, "Truly I say to you, to the extent that you did it to one of these brothers of mine, even the least of them, you did it to Me".
—Matthew 25:34-40 NASB

Jesus truly loved the Father. For Him, it was all about what pleased the Father. He determined to only say what the Father would have Him say. Doing the Father's will was His sustenance, His reason for being. It fed His soul and filled Him with satisfaction. He and His Father had moments of deep communion and intimacy regularly. These were precious moments to Jesus, when the two shared and exchanged from their hearts. His response to the Father's love was to mirror His Father's heart on earth with no personal agenda of His own.

Jesus therefore answered and was saying to them, "Truly, truly, I say to you, the Son can do nothing of Himself, unless it is something He sees the Father *doing; for whatever the* Father *does, these things the Son also does in like manner. For the* Father *loves the Son, and shows Him all things that He Himself is doing; and greater works than these will He show Him, that you may marvel. For just as the* Father *raises the dead and gives them life, even so the Son also gives life to whom He wishes....I can do nothing on My own initiative. As I hear, I judge; and My judgment is just, because I do not seek My own will, but the will of Him who sent Me.*
—John 5:19-21,30 NASB, emphasis mine

That's the kind of love we should be reaching for. We should be seeing the world and everything around us in the light of the Father's vision. Why? Because we and the Father are tight. We know that He loves us and we love Him. Why was Jesus so secure in the knowledge of His

Father's love? Because He had experienced God's love through His awesome blessings. He was constantly speaking of the Father's indulgence, of all the things the Father wanted to do for His children, of all that He was waiting to give to us once we freely came to Him. Because of the Father's generosity, Jesus was spurred to give more freely because He knew His source and place of replenishing. And so Jesus emptied Himself to the point of death, because as His Father mourned for the lost, His heartbeat provoked the Son to secure their restoration.

In this quest to solidify a love relationship with God, it is important to get to His heart. This is where the personality is housed. We have a hard time wrapping our minds around the idea of God having a personality. Often we mistakenly see Him as this huge Omnipresence devoid of feeling. Yet God does have feelings. It is important for us to know how He feels about the world at large, the habits of individuals, the things that make Him angry, the things that make Him sad. We even need to know what makes Him laugh! Yes, God laughs! All of these things are endearing qualities that bring our hearts closer to His.

What is desirable in a man is his kindness.
—Proverbs 19:22 NASB

It is in discovering the soft spots in God's heart that our adoration for Him grows. For us, all of these hints are found in His Word as we read story after story of God's encounters with man throughout the ages. It is not enough to know about God; we must acquire His heart condition. This is how the bond of love grows.

A Change of Heart

Jonah was a prophet who knew how God felt. But when God told him to go and prophesy to Nineveh, he didn't want to go. Nobody liked the Ninevites. They were fearsome, cruel people. Horrendous enemies of Israel. Jonah knew that, in spite of all of this, if he went and prophesied to these people and they repented, God would forgive them. He didn't want God to forgive them. He wanted God to wipe them off the face of the planet! Ever felt like that, wondering why God continues to let some people get away with murder? Well, Jonah wondered, too. True to form, after Jonah ran from God, got swallowed by the whale, and finally gave in to his marching orders, the Ninevites repented and God forgave them. Well, Jonah was fit to be tied. "I knew it!" he said. "I knew You were a gracious and compassionate God, slow to anger and filled with unfailing love. I knew how easily You could cancel Your plans for destroying these people. Just kill me now; I'd rather be dead because nothing I hoped for is going to come true" (see Jonah 4:2,3).

On that note Jonah went and sat down on a hill outside of the city, keeping watch and hoping that God would change His mind. When Nineveh didn't go up in flames, Jonah pouted and fussed at God. But even though he had a bad attitude, God pampered him. He let a plant grow over him for shade and waited for him to see the light, but Jonah was too busy abusing God with his silence. Finally God left him to stew in his own juices and let the plant wither away. When Jonah started to feel sorry for himself, complaining and going through his "woe is me" soliloquy, God chided him on his disposition and asked him how he could care more about a plant than people. "Shouldn't I feel sorry for such a great city?" He asked Jonah. I would've knocked Jonah across the head and said, "Who is God here? You or Me?" But God didn't do that. He understood where Jonah was coming from, but He had a greater plan. So He dealt tenderly with Jonah. He wanted Jonah to understand His heart. And He wants us to understand His heart, too.

And when He saw the multitudes, He went up on the mountain; and after He sat down, His disciples came to Him. And opening His mouth He began to teach them, saying, "Blessed are the poor in spirit, for theirs is the kingdom of heaven. Blessed are those who mourn, for they shall be comforted. Blessed are the gentle, for they shall inherit the earth. Blessed are those who hunger and thirst for righteousness, for they shall be satisfied. Blessed are the merciful, for they shall receive mercy. Blessed are the pure in heart, for they shall see God. Blessed are the peacemakers, for they shall be called sons of God. Blessed are those who have been persecuted for the sake of righteousness, for theirs is the kingdom of heaven. Blessed are you when men cast insults at you, and persecute you, and say all kinds of evil against you falsely, on account of Me. Rejoice, and be glad, for your reward in heaven is great...".
—Matthew 5:1-12 NASB

Jesus was saying that when we adopt God's heart condition, His heart condition, and that of the prophets who had close fellowship with the Father, our reward would be great. What is the reward? God Himself! He says that He will be our exceeding great reward (Genesis 15:1). Can you stand it? Do you realize what that means? When God is your reward, you possess *everything*. Because everything is in Him! Wealth, power, joy, you name it—everything your soul desires is found in the One who created all things, including you.

But in order to claim the reward, we must be tapped in to the spirit and heart of God. This is the heart of an intercessor, who is close to the heart of God, weeping over what He weeps over and rejoicing over what makes Him glad. This is what Jesus, the first intercessor, did for us—did for the world. As He wept over Jerusalem, He continues to weep over all who are lost. As Jesus swept through the temple in righteous indignation casting out the money changers and merchants who had reduced the outer court to a shopping bazaar, He felt the anger His Father felt at this display of total disrespect. The outer court was reserved as the place for the Gentiles to worship. But because the Jews felt that the Gentiles should have no access to their God, they decided to take the outer court and use it for their own gain, for the sale of things for the sacrifice and for foreign exchange. And this made God angry. He had ordained that the entire temple would be sanctified for prayer. What did Jesus say? "It is written, 'My temple shall be a house of prayer, but you have made it a den of thieves'" (see Matthew 21:13). If the Father said it, that was enough for Jesus. His Father's word was the final word. It was God's anger that Jesus felt when He witnessed this blatant disregard for heavenly mandates and went ballistic. We, too, must be indignant against the works of unrighteousness that are committed around us.

For many, being politically correct or seeker-friendly has watered down our strength of conviction. I am always fascinated at how unbelievably considerate we Christians are of others who boldly wave their garbage in our faces, almost daring us to say anything in response. Yet I don't see Jesus compromising the truth anywhere in Scripture. Those who were "seeking" came seeking the truth. They didn't want a watered-down gospel. They had already given up trying to do it their way. They were ready for the unadulterated truth. In other words, they came saying, "Give it to me straight with no chaser!" The sting of truth felt good. That meant the medication was working. Jesus spoke the truth in love to those who were earnestly looking for answers. To water down the gospel message to accommodate another person's comfort level seems to breed more carnality in the church than effective ministry. So while we become more and more seeker-friendly, the world becomes more and more hostile to the things of God and we lose major territory with our empathetic silence. One woman got prayer out of the schools because of her strength of conviction. One woman! If it only takes one person to push the snowball off the side of the mountain and create an avalanche that eventually affects us all, think of what a few bold Christians could do. Look at what twelve men in the book of Acts did. They turned the world upside down!

I am talking about speaking the truth in love here, not about being judgmental, religious, or disdainful. There is a difference. Let's face it. Jesus had no problem with making people upset. They sought to stone Him, they tried to push Him off a cliff, but He wasn't going anywhere until it was His ordained time. He spoke the truth simply and clearly and let the chips fall where they may. The reason no one was able to touch Him before His ordained time was because He did not speak His words; He spoke the words of the Father. The people didn't know who they were messing with! There was no way they could stand up against the power of such an awesome God. It irked them to no end when they couldn't get their hands on Jesus and do Him in. But because He was in the perfect will of the

Father, pursuing the Father's interest, He was untouchable. So if it is fear that is keeping you bound or struggling to make a stand, know that God always has your back if your stand is in accordance with His will.

Consider the things that you allow to slide in your workplace, in your home, in your personal life. Do you really look at the world through the eyes of God? When someone in your office curses, are you so used to it that it rolls off your back as if you were a wet duck? Or does it grieve your spirit and move you to pray for that person or, without being "religious," gently motivate him or her to see how unattractive that kind of speech is? What about when people around you are involved in ungodly behavior? Do you speak the truth to them in love, citing their sin and expressing your concern about them suffering the consequences of their actions? Do you see the people at your job as people who need the Lord, or have you just chalked up what they do to "*those* unsaved people" just being who they are? God didn't put you where you are for nothing. He put you there to effect change. But that will only happen when you begin to see things from His perspective and begin to echo His sentiments to a lost and dying world. Do know that the job does have some perils. Those outside of the body of Christ have the heart of their father and we have the heart of ours—and they are opposite.

If you were of the world, *the* world *would love its own; but because you are not of the* world, *but I chose you out of the* world, *therefore the* world *hates you.*
—John 15:19 NASB, emphasis mine

What Love Does

When we are in love, everything our lover does and says is right. It is all so marvelous to us that we want to share it with everyone so they, too, can partake of the wisdom of our beloved. Jesus came spreading the word of His Father because His Father's heart was His heart. Paul, after being struck down on the road to Damascus, went through a serious attitude adjustment. After his epiphany experience with God, he tapped into His heart. His hatred for Christians was transformed to such a deep degree of love that he became a father to the churches. He wrote letter after letter encouraging the churches in each region to become a body pleasing to God. He was intent on crucifying his own flesh so that God might be the greater voice that was resident within him.

I have been crucified with Christ; it is no longer I who live, but Christ lives in me; and the life which I now live in the flesh I live by faith in the Son of God, who loved me, and delivered Himself up for me.
—Galatians 2:20 NASB, emphasis mine

The love of God within us is going to put some things to death and breathe life into others. It's going to cause us to abhor evil and cleave to that which is good. It is going to cause us to flee lusts, to weep for a dying world, to intercede for the lost, to get rid of our individual prejudices. And it is going to cause God to do some work in us. For instance, God had to straighten Peter out in the book of Acts. God was ready to graft the Gentiles into the family and share with them the fullness of the gospel, but Peter was hesitant because the Gentiles had always been considered unclean. God corrected him, however, and Peter changed his tune as he related this incident to others.

———————————∿∿—————————————

And he said to them, "You yourselves know how unlawful it is for a man who is a Jew to associate with a foreigner or to visit him; and yet God has shown me that I should not call any man unholy or unclean."
—Acts 10:28 NASB

———————————∿∿—————————————

When we love God, we hear His heartbeat clearly. We have teachable spirits that are open to seeing things in a different light—the light of His love and wisdom. Our lives will be transformed as we allow Him to renew our minds. As we absorb His way of thinking, old patterns of habit will fall away and we will discover a whole new brand of liberty—the liberty of man's being one with his Creator.

Remember Shirley with her flaming red jacket? Well, Shirley felt no pain as she stepped beyond the limits of her conservative wardrobe. All she could see was the admiring gaze of her lover. That was her reward. We need to have the same vision. We need to see the admiring gaze of Jesus as we wear His favorite color—the pure white of righteousness—clothed in the beauty of His holiness. And as we look into His eyes, so full of love for us, we will be guided by the light that we see there.

———————————∿∿—————————————

I will instruct you and teach you in the way which you should go; I will counsel you with My eye upon you.
—Psalm 32:8 NASB, emphasis mine

———————————∿∿—————————————

One recent Saturday morning I went out to breakfast and saw all around me couples in love holding hands and talking amongst themselves in soft tones. And each twosome had something in common. No matter what they did, they were constantly looking into one another's eyes. If one looked away, the other turned to follow his or her gaze, unwilling to break the moment of sharing. They wanted to see what the other was seeing. When the waitress approached, two pairs of eyes took in this one figure standing before them. Though only one made a request, the two were in agreement. And everyone around them could feel the intimacy that flowed between them. There was no question about the nature of their relationship. As we look into the eyes of Jesus, we, too, will follow His gaze to see what He sees, simply because that's what lovers do.

On the Love Tip: A Fifth Note

If you fail to see things from God's perspective or have trouble grasping the why of God's Word, I challenge you to ask God to open your eyes, your ears, and your heart to receive His point of view. Begin to see Him as a God with a personality and feelings. Begin to imagine His feelings about specific things that you see, in light of what He had to say about these things in His Word, and take note. Ask Him to convey His heart to you and to share with you the things that burden Him. Open your heart to be used as a conduit of His caring. Ask Him to give you the heart of a true intercessor. Realize that God is just and that all that He does is for our welfare. As your own defenses and rationales are lowered, the understanding of who God is and all that He desires to do for His people becomes amazingly clear. The main directive here is to simply ask God. He says that if any lack wisdom, He will give it to them liberally and will not fuss about it. As He begins to reveal the tenderness of heart He has for others, your own heart will be broken for the world as you come to know His love for you on a whole new level.

Love Note

Because you love My law, you will have great peace.
I will keep you from stumbling.

6
Going Through the Motions

"Ooh! I have to go!" Shirley breathlessly whispered to me over the phone. I rolled my eyes heavenward and chuckled under my breath. It must be HIM again. When I had called moments before, she had set me up for having a short conversation. She was expecting HIM at any moment. And because moments with HIM were deemed precious in her book, I acquiesced to the greater cause of blossoming love, calculating my rising fee for being such an understanding friend. Now that Shirley was deeply entrenched in an official relationship, her time for friends like me was rare. He had become her first priority. When we did get together, we spent countless hours either discussing how giving he was or finding ways to plan pleasant surprises or obtain thoughtful gifts for HIM.

Truly, Shirley was blossoming before my very eyes. Here was a woman who had been extremely self-protective. I must admit that this is my gracious way of saying that the girl had been downright selfish in all of the other romantic relationships I had witnessed her in. But now she was so giving! Not only materially, but truly giving of herself. She was attentive to his every need. She made sure she reserved room for HIM in her otherwise hectic schedule, telling me as if instructing a young pupil, "Quality time with the man you love is important, you know." "Oh," I said, feigning wide-eyed innocence. "He is just something else," she continued. "I feel as if I can't give HIM enough!" Well, this had me completely stymied. "What do you mean by that?" I asked, to which she answered, "He is just so giving, I feel as if I could never repay HIM for all of the things he's done for me." I thought about her answer, then asked, "Why would you want to do that?" I was missing the logic here somewhere. "Michelle, haven't you ever been in love before?" Shirley shook her head at me. And I wondered. I was beginning to think that I hadn't. In fact, I couldn't recall ever having such an acute case of indulgence toward someone else.

By now Shirley was growing impatient with my daftness, so she merely gave a helpless shrug and lectured, "When you truly love someone who is deserving of your love, you will want to give him everything you have—and more—because love can never give enough." What could I say in the face of such profound insight? Those words echoed in my subconscious as Shirley bid me a hasty goodbye now that she was positive it was HIM at her door. I hung up and pondered the benevolence of my own heart. Did I have the right giving attitude toward the Lover of my Soul, or did I give only what I felt like I had to give within the spiritual guidelines? What was my motivation for giving? Tithes? Offerings? My time? Myself? My goals? My desires? All of them seemed to bring a different reaction as I went down the list.

Show Me the Money

Tithing seems to be a favorite subject of most church folk. We ask ourselves a lot of questions about it. To give or not to give? My gross or my net? What about when I am truly broke? On a good day, when I was feeling no lack, I would be quick to answer this question, "Uncle Sam asks for up to thirty-nine point six percent, depending on your tax bracket, and won't give you a dime back. And you're upset because God, who gives you everything, wants a scrawny ten percent?" As I said, that's my reply on a good day. But let's talk about a day when my pocketbook is feeling the pinch. Let's discuss a day when I've fallen a little behind on my bills because I caught a good sale and blew my budget. How cheerful am I about giving then, when it's a choice between the telephone bill and God? Did a hush just descend upon you? You've been guilty too, huh? At least in thought if not in deed. I have to admit that I have grumbled within my spirit from time to time. I sometimes even kinda figure God doesn't even need it. I'm going to have to ask Him for it back somewhere down the line anyway, right? He might as well let me keep it, right? All right, we can repent together!

Perhaps sentiments like these prompted someone to quip that the quickest way to find out if God has your heart is to see if He also has your money. Perhaps this is why Jesus said that it was the *love* of money that was the root of all evil. We serve what we love, that's for sure. We give the object of our affection our all, as Shirley had been quick to sermonize me. And this behavior goes way back. It was what got Cain in trouble. He got in a fight with God over the tithe, got an attitude, and broke fellowship with Him. Over an offering! God was willing to work with Cain. He told him he needed a heart adjustment. God's point was, "My request is reasonable. I want what I want and that's it. If you give it to Me, we can move on and I won't even hold this first faux pas against you." But Cain wanted to do what Cain wanted to do. And wanted God to deal with it. Ain't that special? But we do the same thing. We think God should understand when we spend the money we owe Him on ourselves, but He doesn't. As a matter of fact, He calls it robbery. Look at the last chapter of Malachi for yourself. It's there in big, bold letters, just in case you've gotten convenient amnesia about this whole topic. I'll help you out.

Will a man rob God? *Yet you are robbing Me! But you say, "How have we robbed Thee?" In tithes and offerings.*
—Malachi 3:8 NASB, emphasis mine

God has not asked us to do more than He Himself would do out of His love for us. He has given us everything—including His Only Begotten Son. Nothing was considered too dear to withhold from us. He gave His all to woo us to Himself. Actually, I find it rather gracious of Him to only ask for ten percent. Yet it's enough to cause us all major consternation from time to time. Oh, let's not even bring up offerings above and beyond the ten percent. Some of you might tell me off! I remember going to a church one Sunday and being absolutely fascinated as I watched most of the parishioners put a single dollar bill or some loose change in the offering plate. Later, after finding out that this was the norm in this congregation, I wondered how they could insult God in that way.

For those who use the excuse that they don't know what the pastor is doing with the money, I have one simple answer. It's none of your business. That's between him and God. God holds us responsible for bringing our tithes and offerings to the house of the Lord. We go to restaurants, eat the food, and pay without complaining. (At least, most of the time.) But we understand that we pay for what we get, whether we liked it or not. God feeds us when we come to church. Not only does He feed us with His Word, He feeds us with natural food after we leave church, clothes us, and takes care of our bodies and our minds. He watches over our possessions, and takes care of our families. He listens to us in the midnight hour when everyone else has grown weary of our problems. He provides for us in every way. He blesses us with favor so that we can have a job. He even gives us skills that someone is willing to pay for, and then we balk at giving Him His just desserts. I can only chalk it up to a love problem. Women have willingly given all of their money to men who treated them far worse than God does, and they thought nothing of it.

As the song goes, "You can't beat God giving, no matter how you try." But the question is, do we even attempt to come close? Here was my friend Shirley, trying to find ways to give back to the man in her life half of what he had given her because she was so overwhelmed by his generous nature. As I compared this to the constant outpouring of God in my own life—the immeasurable blessings, the times He touched someone to give me something or led me to a place where I could get what I wanted or needed for a miraculous amount—I had to question the state of my heart and change my attitude about giving. When the devil comes at tax time, prompting me to compare my yearly giving at church to the amount put away in my personal savings account, I should not be moved as I think of the supernatural provision God has made for me over the year. It would definitely add up to much more than I had given. As I began to think along these lines, my heart swelled with love as I considered how indulgent a suitor the Lover of My Soul was. I had story upon story of some special little tidbits and rather large blessings that had come my way in which there was no mistaking the hand of God at work. It made me want to shout! The light went on in my heart. I finally got the full gist of His comment. And then there are the intangibles that we don't readily see, the things we take for granted or things that He provides even though He doesn't have to. I had to come to the conclusion that God doesn't bless us because He *has* to. He blesses us all simply because He *wants* to. And He only asks one small thing of us.

"Bring the whole tithe into the storehouse, so that there may be food in My house, and test Me now in this," says the LORD of hosts, "if I will not open for you the windows of heaven, and pour out for you a blessing until it overflows. Then I will rebuke the devourer for you, so that it may not destroy the fruits of the ground; nor will your vine in the field cast its grapes," says the LORD of hosts.
—Malachi 3:10,11 NASB

Isn't God sweet? He doesn't have to prove Himself to us, and yet He invites us to test Him! I think He understands that this is an area where we all need a little help. We don't trust most people when it comes to our money, and we lump Him in with the rest of those who we fear will take advantage of our giving. When it comes to our finances, we are very much conditioned to fend for ourselves. But here is God promising not only to protect our money from the spirit of robbery, but also to give us a hefty return. Yet for many of us, staring at the bottom line of our savings statement is much safer than taking a gamble on trusting God to be our provider of financial security. Isn't it amazing how crazy we are? We trust airline pilots with our lives more than we trust God. We trust banks to take care of our money, we gamble on the stock exchange every day, we even trust people who can alter our appearance permanently. But when it comes to trusting God to give us a greater return for our money, we just can't see it. He offers a hundred-fold return in provisions and blessings (Mark 10:29, 30). I don't know of any stock that can beat that, yet we hold back, thinking we can handle our money better than the One who created the way to make it in the first place. That's another one of those things that make you go hmm....

Here's how I've changed my tune on giving. The more I fall in love with God, the more I find I want to give to Him. I want to give to further the things that I know are near and dear to His heart. I want to give to my church. I want to give to missions. I want to feed the hungry. I want to send aid to dying children in less fortunate countries. I want to send others who are willing to preach the gospel in those places where I cannot go. Why? Because I know that God cares about these things. I want to make Him smile. I also realize that everything I have belongs to Him. So before I spend a dime of His money, I should make what is important to Him my first priority.

I recall talking to a wealthy friend of mine one day about a designer's line of clothing that we both really liked. We were complaining about her exorbitant prices. I told my friend that I refused to buy any of these clothes no matter how much I loved them simply because it was my way of protesting the cost. But my friend said something that really hit me. "I refuse to spend God's money that way," she said. Wow! I had never looked at it that way! None of what I have really belongs to me. God merely entrusts me to manage it. My friend's statement made so much sense. If I gave someone a huge sum of money and she spent the whole wad on some little self-indulgent trifle, I would be very upset. Yet God is very patient with our unwise spending habits. He watches us pay homage to everyone else—our friends, our homes, our stomachs, our bodies, ourselves. And then we throw Him the leftovers and think He should consider Himself fortunate. Perhaps we don't think of it in such harsh terms, but at the end of the day that's what it boils down to, no matter how much we sugarcoat it. This is one of those areas where we really slide around on His grace. If we saw a man being treated this way by the woman in his life, we would be quick to judge that she was taking terrible advantage of him and that he shouldn't stand for such treatment. Think about it!

Giving God His Due Time

Sometimes I think many of us work so hard that we justify our self-indulgence as our reward for rigorous labor. But ask yourself, *What will I render to God as a reward for all He has done for me?* Truly, the greatest gift besides our tithes, offerings, and resources is our time and ourselves. Many of us do not have enough hours in the day to do all that we need to do. Still, it is important that we give God generous amounts of our time, time a true lover would require in order to keep the relationship alive. Whether the time is spent in service or in prayer, we do ourselves a disservice if we don't give it to Him. I love those bumper stickers that say, "Too busy *not* to pray." It's the truth. Yet the time we siphon out of our busy existences to finish a project or catch up on badly needed rest is the time that should belong to God, the One we cannot afford *not* to interact with.

Recently a friend of mine came to visit me from out of town. We had a hectic weekend of running hither, thither, and yon. On Sunday morning she yawned, stretched out nice and long, and declared that she would skip church and stay home for some extra R & R. She went on to reason that she worked at her church and thus was in church all week long and just needed a break. I was a little amused by this. I thought of David, who was truly in love with God, and his attitude about visiting God's house. He looked forward to seeing God in His house. He went looking for Him; therefore, he had an enthusiasm for making his way into the presence of his God. For David, it was the place of refreshing. No matter how weary he was, he knew that his spirit would be invigorated once he got into the presence of his God.

I was glad *when they said to me, "Let us go to the house of the LORD."*
—Psalm 122:1 NASB, emphasis mine

Though I understood exactly where my dear, exhausted friend was coming from—knew her heart and could even sympathize with her seeming spiritual burnout—I had to challenge her. So I said, "Girl, I know if God were your boyfriend and he had invited you to his house for breakfast, you would be up, dressed, and halfway out the door by now!" On that note, after we had shared a laugh about the truth of my statement, she got up, got dressed, and we both went to church.

The Rest Is on Him

Every day, millions of people get up in the morning and go to a job that they hate, arriving on time whether they are sick, drunk, or crazy. Every Sunday, millions of people roll over in their beds and forsake going to worship the One who is their true provider. Millions face a boss who only cares about what he or she can get while ignoring the One who is constantly thinking of what He can give. Wouldn't you say our priorities are a little bit twisted? None of this is meant to condemn anyone, but we really need to recalibrate our spirits and relocate our center and reason for being. On the flip side of this are all the "religious" churchgoers who go to church out of mere duty and sit like bumps on a log once they arrive. Or they do something worse, offering dried-up worship and warmed-over praise to God. God, however, desires our first fruits—the fresh stuff. Sometimes I wonder if God would prefer for those folks who don't look happy to be in the house of God to just stay at home.

This reminds me of the song where a man is lamenting to his woman that her body is there with him but her mind is on the other side of town. Here is God sitting in heaven seeking worshippers to worship Him in spirit and in truth, and all He gets are a bunch of tired people either falling asleep or praying that the roast doesn't burn before they get back home. Yet if that same church service were a concert with their most-admired artist or a game featuring their favorite athletic team, they would be wide awake and on the edge of their seats, totally into it. The bottom line? We worship what we love. We find the energy to be involved in what we love. We make time for what we love, no matter how exhausted we might be. And still God is gracious, giving us promises to help us every step of the way. It's not a bribe. It's just the essence of His nature to keep giving, to keep meeting us every step of the way.

If thou turn away thy foot from the sabbath, from
doing thy pleasure on my holy day; and call the sab-
bath a delight, the holy of the Lord, *honourable;*
and shalt honour him, not doing thine own ways,
nor finding thine own pleasure, nor speaking thine
own words: then shalt thou delight thyself in the
Lord; *and I will cause thee to ride upon the high*
places of the earth, and feed thee with the heritage of
Jacob thy father: for the mouth of the Lord *hath.*
spoken it.

　　　　　　　　　　　—Isaiah 58:13,14 kjv

God says, "Just give Me one day! One little day!" But now ask me, why does He want that day? Go ahead and ask me, "Michelle, why does God want that one day?" He doesn't want it for Himself, really. He wants *you* to have a day of rest in order to rejuvenate *your* spirit and to refresh *your* mind and body. He wants *you* to be equipped to face the rest of the week. Even God rested from His labor on the seventh day. And what better way to rest than in His presence? He is our rest. Our rest begins with Him, replenishing our spirits with His Word, which is food to our souls! He wants us to stop and refuel with His energizing presence. So even the day He asks for is not requested out of a selfish motive, but as another way of extending His care to us because He loves us so.

He has attached the promise of promotion and prosperity with a day's rest. Why? Because we are able to function more effectively when we take the time to rest and repair our inner man. We return to the workforce invigorated and joyful, ready to be productive. We are well-rested; therefore, we are not on edge, easily offended, or sharp in our interaction with others. Our attitude is one that attracts favor rather than repelling reward. God wants us to be blessed and to be a blessing. Spending time in His presence, resting in His house, refreshing ourselves with a good worship experience, inspires us for the week-long journey through a hostile world. Taking a day to reflect on His care for us rebuilds our security in who we are and *whose* we are. It restores our confidence that we can make it because God is on our side. It reminds us of His promises that we can hold on to in the midst of the challenges that come when we venture out into the world.

I remember that when I was a child, my mother would prepare our Sunday meal on Saturday. As a matter of fact, all work was done on Saturday in preparation for Sunday. Sunday was the day we went to church and just chilled for the rest of the day. On Monday morning I was always refreshed and ready for school. I wasn't worn out from dashing around all over the place both days and having a weekend hangover from overstimulation. Yes, the Lover of Our Souls wants us to come away with Him and partake of delights that set our souls afire and renew our minds. He wants you to rest from your labor and languish in His presence. This is what lovers do. They just like being together. They don't care if the conversation is intriguing or not. It's all about being with the one you love.

Body Language

Don't you just love how we mindlessly sing all those little church songs without thinking about what the words truly say? "Lord, prepare me to be a sanctuary, pure and holy, tried and true....I'm yours, Lord, everything I am, everything I've got...try me now and see if I can be completely yours...." A lot of us would be in trouble if God took us up on some of the promises we sing to Him. Promises of yielding all that we are to Him. The kind of promises He loves and wishes that we would truly deliver. We all sing these songs with the best of intentions, yet it is important for us to follow through in order to reap the total benefits of our love relationship with God. True lovers want to give their bodies to their lover. They want their bodies to be pleasing to the object of their affection. And Paul told us we were to give our bodies back to God.

I beseech you therefore, brethren, by the mercies of God, that ye present your bodies a living *sacrifice, holy, acceptable unto God, which is your reasonable service.*

—Romans 12:1 KJV, emphasis mine

"This is only *reasonable*," he said. This shouldn't be a difficult thing for you, considering He made your body in the first place. It would be like refusing to return a vase to the potter who made it. How do you say no to the creator? But even deeper, how do you say no to the One who loves you because you are His handiwork? The One who knows exactly how many hairs are on your head? Who knows your inner parts? How do you say no when He asks for your arms to hold someone who's hurting? How do you say no when He asks you to go to those who need help? How do you resist the call of the One who made you to use what He gave you for His service? Or merely to take better care of it for your own sake?

I thought about Shirley, a woman who always insisted on knowing what was on her calendar weeks in advance. Now that she was involved with HIM, whenever he called, no matter how impromptu the moment, she was available. And though I don't recommend that single women be too readily available at all times, I do recommend it if the Man calling is the Lord Jesus. He deserves our constant availability because He is always beside us. His ear is always open to our cry, no matter what time day or night. He continually watches over us. He never slumbers or sleeps, so diligent is His care over us.

Paul calls making our bodies available to God an act of worship. It is the last reserve of what we cling to. After all, our bodies belong to us. Or so we think. Actually, they don't. We've been bought with a price. Christ gave His body for ours, and yet we continue to cling to ourselves even while we ignore the precious treasure that we have within us—the Holy Spirit Himself. This is a good enough reason to take better care of our bodies. We need to watch what we eat, monitor how we dress, and be aware of what we submit our bodies to. We need to avoid what is not healthy for us physically, emotionally, or spiritually. To do anything less would be like taking an expensive gift someone gave you and smashing it on purpose right before their very eyes. Think of how they would feel, knowing you thought so little of the great expense they went to in order to bless you. Remember that old song where the girl told her love to button up his overcoat? She said, "Take good care of yourself. You belong to me." Well, that's how God feels about us.

But not only has God chosen to bless us with the body we have; He has chosen to live inside the gift He's given us in the person of His precious Holy Spirit! That's what we need to cling to. He resides within us, patiently counseling us every step of the way, leading and directing, making God's presence and watchfulness known in countless ways. Oh, yes, it is time to give it up. Many a woman has given her body, her soul, her everything, to a man who loved her less. As I sit and consider all that God has done out of His great love for me, I must mirror the words of the psalmist: "What shall I render to the Lord for all His benefits toward me?" Truly, everything we are, everything we have, is not enough.

On the Love Tip: Six Down

If you're struggling with giving your tithes or resenting being asked to give offerings above your tithes, go through your closets. Consider your favorite pieces of furniture and art and see them in a new light. See them as presents from the Lover of Your Soul. Now consider how much it would cost you to match the sum total of all those presents and choose to give your tithe cheerfully. If you hoard your time for yourself or feel that your body is yours to do with as you please, try this exercise. Monitor a day when you spend your first time of the day with the Lord versus a day when you don't and judge your level of effectiveness. I can tell you already which day will be a better one. Begin to take care of your body the way you would as if you were preparing to meet the love of your life who was coming home after a long journey because guess what? You are. If going to church is a dry experience for you, it's time for a love boost. First, you must learn to consider every moment spent with God as a special date. Anticipate seeing Him when you go to His house. Turn your attention away from the service and all that comes with going through the motions of worship. Begin to literally respond to His presence before you. Reach out to Him and feel Him touch you back. Praise Him and see Him appreciate your worship. Stretch beyond your senses, move past your brain to the place where your spirit is free to reach the heavens. Capture the moment and hold it as long as you can. I guarantee it will only be enough to keep you longing for more.

Love Note
Remember, I loved you first.

7

Charity Begins at Heart

I have to stop by the cleaners for HIM," Shirley said as we turned the corner. "Okay," I replied, matching her stride. "Hey, what are you doing this weekend? I thought maybe we could raid the outlet mall." I saw a spark of delight light up Shirley's eyes. "Ooh, that would be fun! Hey, don't they have an amusement center there? The kids would love it!" *Wait a minute!* I thought. *What is Shirley talking about?* "Whoa!" I exclaimed. "What kids?" She shrugged. "Oh, I'm watching his sister's kids this weekend. She and her husband need a break." I stopped in the middle of the sidewalk, ignoring the crowd around me. "You don't even *like* kids, Shirley. What are you talking about?" She simply smiled. "I like his sister's kids. They're so cute!" I was still unconvinced. "Cute enough to jump all

105

over your white couch?" I knew how much my friend loved that couch. "Oh, what's a couch?" Shirley waved away my comment and resumed walking. "Besides, I'll only have them one day. I promised his mom I'd come over to help her cook for his dad's birthday party on Sunday." Well, if you had blown on me I would have fallen over! "Do you even know how to cook?" I pinched her to see if I was still talking to the Shirley I knew. The Shirley who only ordered in or did carry-out food—or went out to eat. "Of course, silly! And I'm good, too." She laughed at my concern. "But you never cook," I challenged. "Why should I?" she replied. "It's boring when you're just cooking for yourself." I thought about it for a moment. "I see…"

Funny how love will cause you to embrace the most insignificant of tasks with delight. No wonder the psalmist had no problem with the thought of being a doorkeeper in the house of the Lord.

For a day in Thy courts is better than a thousand outside. I would rather stand at the threshold of the house of my God, than dwell in the tents of wickedness.
    —Psalm 84:10 NASB

Here was a man who considered it a privilege to be a servant in the house of the God he served. If he had to be an usher, he considered it an honor. He would rather work in the house of the Lord than languish in a place where God's Spirit could not be found. I thought of the many churches I have visited on a regular basis during my ministerial travels. I thought of the faithful ladies who set up the church platform each Sunday, and of the men who faithfully moved the equipment and kept the church clean. The number was far too few. I was able to confirm that the same people diligently went about their work week in and week out because there were not enough volunteers to rotate the duties. On the other hand, the praise and worship teams brimmed over with singers. The liturgical dancers overflowed the stage. It seemed that everyone wanted the high-profile jobs. Teaching children's church and working in the nursery followed the same order as the tasks of cleaning and setting up the church. No one wanted to skip a service to be tucked away on the sidelines, missing out on all of the action. So many who had gifts that would really bless the congregation continued to sit unmoved as appeals were made for church workers. I found it all very interesting—and disturbing—and wondered what the problem was. But, as always, it boiled down to one thing—love.

Dressing for the Part

I think we've gotten distracted by all the activity that takes place in church. It's become a gas station of sorts. We drag in empty, plopping down, folding our arms, and saying in our minds, "Okay, let me hear something to make me feel better. Fill me up. Entertain me. Make me say, 'Hmm, that's deep.' Titillate my intellect. Satisfy my flesh." We never stop to think that *we* are supposed to bring something to the party. This is because we think we are simply going to church. But we need to remember we are going to the King's house! Not just any king, but the KING of KINGS. We should be like the little drummer boy in the Christmas carol who couldn't bear to go see the baby Jesus without having a gift to present to Him. When he found he had nothing material to share, he gave all he had—a song. And not just any song. His best song. In many cultures it is considered bad manners to enter someone else's house without bringing something to drink or some other gift to show the host your appreciation for being invited. You are expected to come dressed in your best, bringing your best. Yet we forget that we should feel honored to enter God's house. We come to *be* served rather than *to serve*. But all of that is made clear when we are in love.

I thought of the sweet little ladies who regularly served at my church. Of the tender care they gave to every detail of what they were doing. The flowers had to be just so. I would catch them removing imaginary dust from a chair. There was love in every one of their actions. These ladies had the love light of God shining in their eyes and their dispositions were as sweet as sugar. Doing what they did was an automatic reaction because they were taking care of His house. And they loved every minute of it because they loved Him.

When Queen Esther went to see the king, she prepared herself by putting on beautiful robes that were pleasing to his eye. Though she had a desperate need, she made sure she first served the king before presenting her problem to him. A smart woman knows she gets more out of a man when he is satisfied than when he is distracted by dissatisfaction and lack. We all could take a lesson from Esther. Perhaps this is why when Jesus taught us to pray, He recommended that we start with praise and worship to God, then wind our way toward presenting our needs. We are always far more willing to help those who appreciate us.

I love Esther's story because I think it speaks volumes about how to get the King's attention and have our own needs fulfilled. First, it says that Esther fasted and prayed. She got self out of the way before she went in to see the king. She crucified the flesh so that she could be tuned into anything she needed to hear that could help her dire situation. Now, all of us are not going to fast every time before we go to church, but perhaps we *can* silence our flesh. We can decide to go seeking what God has to say before seeking our own agendas. Sometimes we're so busy listening for the answer to our problem that we miss it. We miss it because we get focused on a specific way our prayer should be answered and God is coming from a whole different direction that offers greater liberation.

Getting back to Esther, though. The next thing she did was to get dressed in royal garments. Now, this might be my own personal nit so don't get sensitive on me, but I'm sorry. Sometimes I wonder what people are thinking when they get dressed for church. If you were going to a function to meet the President of the United States, you would not show up in something you would wear to a picnic. You would dress respectably because you respect his office. Yet we have this casual mentality about going to see the King. The reality of who we are going to see is not quite real enough to us, in my opinion. Ask yourself this question. If you knew that Jesus was going to be at your church in bodily form so that you could see Him, how would you dress? I can hear some of you grumbling already, "But we're supposed to come to Him as we are!" That's true. Come as you are *inside*. A sinner in search of grace. Remember, God loves us enough to invite us as we are, but He loves us too much to leave us in our old condition. That's why we are urged to have our lives transformed by the renewing of our minds. Oh, and I know the other argument, too: "Well, God knows what's in my heart." Uh-huh...and it shows, 'cause He said, "As a man or woman thinks in his or her heart so is he or she." That means whatever you're thinking shows in your actions—in this specific case, by what you say, do, and *wear*. When you're on your way to see someone important, you don't dress as if you're doing yardwork or going on a hike. You come "correct," as they say in Urbanese. Your respect for God will show in all of these areas, thus revealing your true state of heart. Think about it.

So does God really care about what you wear to church? I think He does. He was awfully fussy about what the priests wore when they came into His presence to minister. He spent several days discussing this whole dressing thing with Moses up on the mountain. The priests were not to come bopping into the Holy of Holies looking any ole how; they had to come clean. They came looking as if they had been set apart from the masses who approached God, set apart from any other ordinary activity. Going to see God was not to be confused with going to the market. It was exhibiting spiritual discipline to go before the Lord dressed appropriately in reverence of His holiness. Now we are all called to be priests unto God. Everything we do or say has a spiritual connection, including how we dress.

I'm not picking on your clothing for nothing. I just want you to get a revelation of its importance on two levels. First, when we take care in how we dress when we go to see God, it is a sign of honor to Him. Secondly, dressing nicely makes us carry ourselves differently in His presence. You know how we are. Our whole body language changes according to how we are dressed. When we are in sweats and T-shirts, we slouch and sit any ole kind of way. You know what I'm talking about! But put on a dress and a pair of heels and we've got a whole different thing going on. We stand taller and our countenance changes. Our posture and behavior rise to another level. We move with more grace. And put on some lipstick and do your hair...well! Now you are something else!

I thought of my friend Shirley, who I often found hanging around in her faded jeans, favorite comfy shirt on, tails hanging out. At least, this is how she was until she heard HIM pulling into her driveway. In one instant, or so it seemed, a complete transformation would take place. She would dash to her room and find some simple yet classy thing to slip into. A spritz of perfume and a dab of lipstick later, this elegant woman would emerge from her bedroom door to greet HIM whom her soul loveth. No more ratty jeans or old shirts. Girlfriend was refined. She wanted to be at her best in her man's presence. And we should be that way in God's presence. You see, casual dress in church quite often makes us carry an air of casual familiarity that borders on disrespect. Remember, the fear of the Lord is the beginning of wisdom (Job 28:28). Though the veil of separation has been rent allowing us free access to God, we still must walk in an attitude of reverence before Him. The place where He dwells is holy ground. If He doesn't care what we wear in His presence, why did He tell Moses to remove his sandals? He didn't want anything dirty and worn to defile the place of His holiness.

Be silent, all flesh, before the LORD; for He is
aroused from His holy habitation!
—Zechariah 2:13 NASB, emphasis mine

When people in the Bible witnessed the presence of the Lord, they generally bowed down, were silent and trembled, so awesome was His presence in their midst. Yet here we come schlepping to God, giving Him a high-five, practically saying, "Hey, dude!" It is the fine line a teenager draws between his parent being his parent, versus being his friend. We must be careful. We are His children who must come before Him with hearts of worshippers. True worshippers think of serving more than of being served. Their hearts wait upon the Lord.

Behold, as the eyes of servants look to the hand *of their master, as the eyes of a maid to the* hand *of her* mistress; *so our eyes look to the* LORD *our God, until He shall be gracious to us.*
—Psalm 123:2 NASB, emphasis mine

Esther came seeking to serve the king before seeking his aid. She gave great thought to how she looked, how she carried herself, and how she approached the king. It moved his heart to embrace her. He wanted to bless her with riches. While the king offered Esther up to *half* of his kingdom, it is our heavenly Father's desire to give us the *whole* kingdom when we are pleasing to Him. Esther pleased the king and he went beyond the call of duty to give her the desire of her heart—and more. There will always be an overflow of blessings when we come into God's presence seeking to satisfy Him and serve Him first before we seek to help ourselves.

Esther even served her enemy before she got around to seeking help for herself, and in the end the king rose to her defense and destroyed her foe. Now, that's a powerful lesson on service. When Esther lost herself in the pleasure of utilizing all of her talents to serve her king, he took care of all concerning her, right down to getting rid of anything that threatened to rob her of her security and well-being. She was well taken care of in the end. If a human understands giving and taking on that level, how much more will God understand it and bless you?

The Proof Is in the Pudding

Jacob worked for the hand of Rachel for seven years, got duped by her father, and worked another seven years, so determined was he to be with the woman he loved. The Bible says that the time seemed as a day to him, so great was his love for Rachel. I find it interesting that it never occurred to Jacob that he should be able to get Rachel without having to invest anything. To him, it was a given that love means giving of yourself in service as an act of commitment. In the end, God honored Jacob's work by increasing him on every side. He left the house of Rachel's father a rich man with the woman he loved as well as servants and livestock that rivaled what his father-in-law owned. Jacob didn't go looking to get something for nothing and, because of his attitude, he walked away with more than he imagined.

As we determine to come to church as worshipers and servants in God's house, God meets us in countless ways. Jacob was happy to serve Rachel's family because he was in love with Rachel. When we are in love with God, we find joy in serving everyone connected to Him as well. As we begin to use our talents to bless God's people and to glorify Him, He increases our talents and opens richer doors of opportunity for us. This usually spills over into increase— spiritually, emotionally, and financially. Our joy increases. A sense of purpose is born. We can feel and see the evidence of moving in the center of God's will for our lives. Because we are in love, every task, no matter how great or small, becomes honorable because the motivation to set our hands to work is borne out of love for God. Working in the church nursery takes on a whole new glow as we see all of those babies as God's precious little lambs. All of those rambunctious children to be taught in Sunday school become little jewels filled with the potential to really shine for God. And you're responsible for bringing out the glow in their tiny spirits! Sweeping the floors and vacuuming the carpets takes on a whole different meaning when you think of keeping *His house* clean as opposed to cleaning *the church*. You'll find yourself doing things that are not your responsibility simply because it's all about *Him* and what He delights in, versus you and what is, or isn't, in your job description.

When we are earthbound, everything brings us down. This is why we are called to look up. And looking up goes beyond the walls of the church to the places where we work every day. There is so much mediocrity in the workplace, even among Christians, because we all get so locked into focusing on the mortal man we are serving rather than seeing the One we really work for.

Slaves, obey your earthly masters with respect and fear, and with sincerity of heart, just as you would obey Christ. Obey them not only to win their favor when their eye is on you, but like slaves of Christ, doing the will of God from your heart. Serve wholeheartedly, as if you were serving the Lord, not men, because you know that the Lord will reward everyone for whatever good he does, whether he is slave or free.
—Ephesians 6:5-8 NIV

Even in the marketplace, it is Christ we work for. We should serve cheerfully and with excellence because we love Christ and want to represent Him well. Our goal should be for men to see our good works and glorify our Father in heaven. However, the world is no longer service-oriented because, for the most part, we as a people have become lovers of ourselves. We are self-motivated, instead of being God-inspired. "What am I going to get out of it?" is the mantra of today. But you'll only ask this question if you don't truly understand God's heart. The more that we pour out to Him, the greater the magnitude that He pours out in abundant measure. He is a firm believer in reciprocation. I have learned from experience that, as I willingly serve others, God sends people into my life to serve me. It also opens the door for greater opportunities in my life. I truly believe that as I served my cousin and assisted him in his ministry, I received an impartation of his anointing that prepared me for my own ministry. God honored my service by promoting me in due season. Truly, the way up is down.

May I Help You?

On the other hand, to walk in the attitude that service is beneath you—even though the truth of the matter is that we all have to serve somebody—is to set yourself up to be robbed of blessings. I have a confession to make. There have been days when I have gone to a store and been so turned off by the attitude of the sales clerk that I have deliberately not purchased something simply because I didn't want that person to get the sales commission. She behaved as if she were doing me a favor as opposed to having an attitude of service. I have found this rather distasteful and therefore have refused to reward those who behaved as if they were paying me when it was really the other way around. Anybody know what I'm talking about here?

I have also sat in restaurants where the waiter acted as if he were doing me a favor by serving me the food I was paying for. Instead of leaving a monetary tip, I have left a written tip, offering the advice that when he changed his attitude, he would receive the fifteen-percent gratuity he felt it was my duty to leave him. Can you second the motion? I imagine this is how God feels sometimes. I am sure this is why He says that a haughty spirit goes before a fall. We lose out every time. Ah, but when *we* humble *ourselves!* Yes, we should humble ourselves before someone does it for us. Then God will lift us up. On the other hand, I have had waiters serve me who were so gracious that my companion and I have said to each other, "He was really good. We have to leave him a good tip." And we do! When we get over ourselves, we are put in the position to be blessed over and above our expectations.

When we are in love with God, we want to serve His people. That's the bottom line. As we immerse ourselves in serving first the household of faith, our spirits are enriched and we are built up in our inner man. This insulates our hearts from offense and we are then able to serve the world at large freely. As we joyfully serve those who are seemingly unworthy, God is glorified. Those we consider enemies are then humbled beneath the mighty hand of God. We don't have to do it; God does it for us. They will either bow beneath the hand of God and come to the place of repentance, or be broken, period.

If we consider the role of a servant, two things become clear. One, servants know that they have no rights except those which the master gives them. Two, they know that their duty is to anticipate the needs of the master alone. That is it. Dwelling on what we consider to be our rights will kill the spirit of service. This is what got Satan in trouble. The love of himself rose above love for God and he decided that all the worship should come to him instead of to God. The minute he attempted to grasp what belonged to God and claim his own rights, he got in trouble and lost it all. I don't think he realized he had been sitting pretty until he found himself plummeting downward out of the heavens. As Paul said, we were dead and our lives are now hidden in Christ. So much for our rights. They are hidden in Christ, too. If we are dead, we can't insist on anything, can we? Attention, respect...any of the things we think we are justified in receiving. I once heard a preacher say, "A dead man won't rise up in his casket if someone spits on him because he is dead." He is dead to offense, dead to robbery. If you decided to steal something off that body, it wouldn't rise up and say, "That belongs to me." It is dead. A true servant is dead to his own desires. But that is the place we all must arrive at in order to receive.

For whoever wants to save his life will lose it, but whoever loses his life for me will save it.
—Luke 9:24 NIV, emphasis mine

This is the true heart of a servant. Jesus was our greatest example. His truest act of servanthood was to lay down His life for us. He served His Father, anticipating His every wish all the way to the cross. So deep was His love for the Father that nothing else mattered. All He knew was how God felt about us. How desperately He longed for us to be redeemed. On that note, He took off His own royal robes to come after us and pay the ransom to bring us back to God. This is the attitude we need to imitate as we consider serving those around us.

Let this mind be in you, which was also in Christ Jesus: Who, being in the form of God, thought it not

robbery to be equal with God: But made Himself of
no reputation, and took upon him the form of a ser-
vant, and was made in the likeness of men: And being
found in fashion as a man, he humbled himself, and
became obedient unto death, even the death of the
cross. Wherefore God also hath highly exalted him,
and given him a name which is above every name.
                              —Philippians 2:5-9 KJV

So why is service so important if Jesus has seemingly done it all? Because He still wants to perfect those of us who remain on the earth into Oneness. It is only in serving God that we become One with Him as we partner in the things that His heart beats for. It is in serving others that our unity on earth is solidified. In order to serve, you must get beneath a person and literally carry him to the place of fulfilling his need. No one fights a person who is carrying him. He relaxes and molds himself to the form of the other in order to remain secure; otherwise, he would fall and hurt himself. It is instinctual that his arms will wrap around you to steady himself. It is this molding together in the spirit that God is after. We will never be able to embrace the concept of being a servant as long as we conclude that humility is weakness. Jesus didn't feel that anything was beneath Him because He understood fully who He was and who He served. No external act could change that. Therefore, He was able to lower Himself because He understood He was already exalted.

Jesus knowing that the Father had given all things
into his hands, and that he was come from God, and
went to God; he riseth from supper, and laid aside his

garments; and took a towel, and girded himself. After
that he poureth water into a bason, and began to wash
the disciples' feet, and to wipe them with the towel
wherewith he was girded. Then cometh he to Simon
Peter: and Peter saith unto him, Lord, dost thou wash
my feet? Jesus answered and said unto him, What I do
thou knowest not now; but thou shalt know hereafter.
Simon Peter saith unto him, Lord, not my feet only,
but also my hands and my head. Jesus saith to him,
He that is washed needeth not save to wash his feet,
but is clean every whit: and ye are clean, but not all.
—John 13:3-10 KJV

Sometimes others will get the wrong impression as we
humble ourselves to serve them. Don't worry about it. Let
them! It's not about them. It's not about you. But it *is* all about
God. Those who are important to Him must be important to
us if we're truly in love with the Lover of Our Souls. We will
want to serve His family. We will want to serve those who He
longs to make a part of the family, no matter how unlovable
they might be. He loves them, and that should be enough for
us. So how do we accomplish getting past ourselves, past the
bad attitudes of others, and into His heart? Through the
giving of our gifts and talents, a loving attitude, a humble disposition, and our acts of service. (To me, that is a kinder word
than *work*.) First to Him, and then to others. Remember, to
serve others is to serve God. To serve God is an act of worship
and a confirmation of our devotion to Him. The more we do
it, the more enjoyable it becomes as we begin to experience
the blessings that come our way when we choose to serve for
no other reason than because we are in love.

On the Love Tip: In the Seventh Inning

If you are struggling with the concept of humility and service, consider Jesus. As you think about what He did for your sake, consider all He left behind in order to win you. Think about how He pursued you and about what those around you mean to Him. Make a list of all the ways that He serves you. Now think of an area where you can be of service to Him. The clue will be in the needs of those around you. Think of the Lord as a potential employer and fill out a job application. You must list the position you want, explain why it is important to you, and state your qualifications. Determine how this position will be of help to Him and figure out how your work would benefit the Kingdom. As you begin to see what you have to offer as a gift that contributes to God's Kingdom design, your attitude toward serving will be transformed. You will be able to find joy in doing your work as unto the Lord. Your heart will be knit closer to His as you become a willing partner with Him in establishing His purposes in the earth.

Love Note

I will serve you in the presence of your enemies. I will anoint your head with oil and cause your cup to run over.

8

That Lovin' Feelin'

"He must be having a bad day," Shirley said thoughtfully as we left the store. I'd thought the clerk was downright rude. But Shirley had exercised great patience as this man with an obvious chip on his shoulder continued to be as caustic as ever in the face of Shirley's gentle demeanor. And my friend was surprisingly unfazed by it all. As a matter of fact, she dealt with this sourpuss with a great degree of compassion. I knew that Shirley had the capacity to put someone in his place in a minute if he stepped out of line, but not today. "How could you let him talk to you like that?" I was indignant even though I was not the one who had been addressed. "Oh, girl," she answered, "I'm not about to let that old man faze me. I'm too happy to let him rain on my parade. Poor guy...." On that note, she began humming. "Isn't it just the most beautiful day you've ever seen?" Her voice was musical with delight, but I was still a bit off-balance from our entire encounter with Mr. Chip-on-His-Shoulder. "Mmm..." I mumbled as Shirley jabbed me playfully with her elbow and chided, "Oh, snap out of it! You're not going to let Mr. Grumpy ruin your day, are you? We've got better things to do. Come on, put some pep in your step." Of course! How could I be so daft? No wonder Shirley was so unmoved by this unpleasant experience. She had no time to linger on unpleasantries. She was on her way to see HIM.

Funny thing about love. It truly insulates the heart from offense. You are unable to stay angry because you have greater things to think about. The more your heart burns with love and passion for someone in your personal world, the more oblivious you will be to the irritating trifles of life and the lapses of kindness around you. Those negative things become peripheral afterthoughts. But what about someone like myself who is not in love with anyone? Who has no man in my life causing me to arise with a song in my heart each morning? What source do I draw from for the kind of love that keeps me in such a positive state of mind that I am able to ward off the abrasiveness of people caught up in their own personal dramas? Why, the only source of constant love that remains unchanging—God.

Spread the Love

This even holds true for those who are in love, in committed relationships, or married. As we know, the love gauge in human relationships goes up and down based on shifting circumstances and experiences. Therefore, one invariable source is needed to keep our hearts fixed. That source has to be God. God is love. If He lives inside of us, we know what to do on those days when our flesh gets in the way of that lovin' feelin'. All we have to do is let Him come out and do His thing. His love will fill in the gaps our emotions leave empty. His love at work within us helps us to love the lovable, the unlovable, and those in between. Not only does it make the negative bounce off of our hearts, it also pumps up the positive. Love makes you generous and more sensitive to those around you. God so loved us that He pressed past being turned off by our state of sin and gave His Only Begotten Son to *everybody*. He wanted to spread the love! To share His good thing with us!

I have a girlfriend who shared with me that her capacity to love her husband, as wonderful as he was, was in direct relationship to how she felt about God. When her love relationship with God was intact and brimming over, she felt an increase of love toward her mate. But when she was running on low with God, her love meter for her husband hovered near empty. Why? Because her love source had been cut off. Consider what happens when you step on a hose when the lawn sprinkler is on. The flow of water stops and is unable to get through to dampen the earth. But when the hose is clear, refreshing comes to the earth, the grass grows, and even the air is affected by the presence of that beautiful greenery. Likewise, everyone and everything is affected by love. It is the driving force behind the well-being of everything on the face of the earth. When love is not present, greed, strife, and evil works are unleashed—adultery, robbery, even war. Cities are devastated and people die because of this. It is a sin not to love. And the end of sin is always death. And yet without the knowledge of God, we are incapable of love. If we don't know Him, we can't love Him. If we can't love Him, we are unable to love others

---

Beloved, let us love one another, for love is from God; and everyone who loves is born of God and knows God. The one who does not love does not know God, for God is love....Whoever confesses that Jesus is the Son of God, God abides in him, and he in God. And we have come to know and have believed the love which God has for us. God is love, and the one who abides in love abides in God, and God abides in him....We love, because He first loved us. If someone says, "I love God," and hates his brother, he is a liar; for the one who does not love his brother whom he has seen, cannot love God whom he has not seen. And this commandment we have from Him, that the one who loves God should love his brother also.

—1 John 4:7,8,15,16,19-21 NASB

We know love by this, that He laid down His life for us; and we ought to lay down our lives for the brethren.

—1 John 3:16 NASB, emphasis mine

God says He deposited love into our accounts, and we owe Him a balance. He has chosen to diversify our love account, dividing it between Himself and those around us. This is our way of reflecting Him to the world. It helps others to see the Kingdom of God in a good light and become attracted to the King. Doesn't make sense yet? Think of the opposite. What does the world say when people who call themselves Christians are at odds with one another? Whether they are disputing theology and doctrines or killing innocent people in the name of God, they all get lumped together in the same synopsis. Those outside of the body decide they want no part of Christianity if such awful behavior is any indication of what life in the Kingdom is all about. They see no need for God if this is how we behave. Funny, sometimes the world knows better than we do that Christians are supposed to be loving. Let's face it, whether we believe it or not, we are responsible for guarding the reputation of God's family. We are called to live lives that are sanctified, set apart for the glory of God, making a difference in the earth.

Sanctify them through thy truth: thy word is truth. As thou hast sent me into the world, even so have I also sent them into the world. And for their sakes I sanctify myself, that they also might be sanctified through the truth.

—John 17:17-19 KJV

Even Jesus sanctified Himself for our sakes, died, rose, ascended into heaven, and passed the torch on to us to carry on the tradition of glorifying the Father through our actions and our love toward one another. This is the greatest witness we have.

By *this all men will* know *that you are My disciples, if you have* love *for one another.*

—John 13:35 NASB, emphasis mine

By *this we* know *that we* love *the children of God, when we* love *God and observe His commandments.*

—1 John 5:2 NASB, emphasis mine

When we walk in submission to God, allowing the spirit of love to reign within us, we recognize that spirit in others. Everyone can relate to being somewhere and meeting total strangers but instantly liking them for absolutely no reason at all. And then somewhere along the way in conversation, you find out they are Christians. Based on that knowledge, you totally embrace them. You have Someone in common. "You know Jesus? Hey, I know Him too! Isn't He wonderful?" Because you have a shared love, it opens the door to friendship, the type of friendship that causes us to cleave to one another, to become united in spirit. It is this unity that dismantles lack in our lives. This is what took place in the book of Acts. The people were bonded together in the unity of faith, and they had all things in common. They sold all they had and pooled their resources for the common good of all. There were no haves and have-nots. There was no such thing as "my own space" or "my exclusive stuff." No competition among them. They all shared and shared alike. There was no need for a governmental welfare system because everyone looked out for the welfare of the other. Widows and children were high on the list of priority, and because of their care for one another, they were a community that was thriving and growing strong.

Theirs was a testimony to the provision of God. David said that he had never seen the righteous out begging for bread. Why? Because God's people took care of their own—and everyone else in need, too, for that matter. A true Christian understands that everyone matters to God. Based on our love for Him, that love extends to all others His heart beats for.

A Love Decision

I find it interesting that we are commanded to love God with all our heart, soul, mind, and strength, but to love our neighbor as we love ourselves. Notice we are not commanded to love ourselves. This is something that we just automatically do. As a matter of fact, we can love ourselves to a fault in God's eyes. We can love ourselves more than we love Him, and that puts us in real trouble. We are commanded to love God with everything we have within us, but exhibit the same care toward our neighbor that we would for ourselves. I wonder why we weren't commanded to love our neighbor as we love God? Perhaps God, in His foreknowledge of our heart condition, knew that He could bank on the love we had for ourselves more than the love we had for Him. That's a sad commentary. But then Christ came on the scene and told everybody they had to get over themselves, that to seek to save their own lives was to lose them, and that selfishness was out and giving was in. He now added Himself to the mix as an example of the type of love we should have for our neighbor by adding a new commandment.

A new commandment I give to you, that you love one another, even as I have loved you, that you also love one another. By this all men will know that you are My disciples, if you have love *for one another.*
—John 13:34,35 NASB, emphasis mine

Greater love *has no one than this, that one lay down his life for his friends*
—John 15:13 NASB, emphasis mine

"What, God?" you may ask. *"You want me to be willing to give my life for people?"* His reply is "yes" in the literal and not-so-literal sense. He wants us to put other people's needs

before our own desires. *"But isn't that going a little too far?"* you respond. *"This is not a society where it is considered wise to be self-sacrificing. People will take advantage of me. Where is the line drawn between being a good, loving, giving Christian and an all-out fool?"* Allow God to draw that line for you as you follow His example.

But I say to you who hear, love *your enemies, do good to those who hate you*
—Luke 6:27 NASB, emphasis mine

And if you love *those who* love *you, what credit is that to you? For even sinners* love *those who* love *them.*
—Luke 6:32 NASB, emphasis mine

But love *your enemies, and do good, and lend, expecting nothing in return; and your reward will be great, and you will be sons of the Most High; for He Himself is kind to ungrateful and evil men.*
—Luke 6:35 NASB, emphasis mine

Now, is that deep or what? It's one thing to overcome the disappointment of someone doing you wrong, but to knowingly be kind to those who you know are your enemies is something else! Yet this is what Christ did. Now that He lives in us, we are called to an even higher order of love, above what comes naturally to us. We are called to love as He loved, and His love covers a multitude of our sins. Whenever doing this becomes difficult, just think back on your own life. When you didn't care about Christ, He was still caring for you, watching over you, looking out for you. Still doing things on your behalf while you continued to ignore Him. He was a gentle lover in pursuit of you as His prize, and no level of indifference on your behalf could deter Him from reaching out to you. We are to have that same determined love for others, and eventually love will triumph.

Love is patient, love is kind, and is not jealous; love does not brag and is not arrogant. It does not act unbecomingly; it does not seek its own, is not provoked, does not take into account a wrong suffered, does not rejoice in unrighteousness, but rejoices with the truth; bears all things, believes all things, hopes all things, endures all things. Love never fails....

—1 Corinthians 13:4-8 NASB

Actions Speak Louder Than Words

So how do we love God in light of the love chapter (1 Corinthians 13)? Does that passage also apply to loving Him? I think it does. Let's take a look. Loving God with all we have within us means we will be patient with His plan for our lives, even when we don't understand what the wait is all about. Are we ever unkind to God? I think we are. I don't think any of us escapes from wondering about His motives toward us. Can you imagine how that hurts His heart? When we wonder if He gives preferential treatment to some or covet the blessings He has given to others, this is being jealous. When we claim credit for the blessings He has given us, that is the height of arrogance. Sin is unbecoming. Our refusal to surrender our lives and our will to Him is completely self-seeking. To accuse God of not granting you the desires of your heart or of withholding blessings you've asked for is to accuse Him of wrongdoing. To tolerate or compromise in the midst of unrighteousness is to rejoice in it. Remember, making no decision means that you've made a decision. To say nothing does not mean you oppose what you witness. Because we love Him, we rejoice when people do the right thing. We acknowledge and celebrate their right choices. We are able to bear all things for the sake of Christ because His burden is light. Like Paul, we pick up our cross daily and follow Him. We continue to hope in God because His Word is true. We continue to believe Him in the face of seemingly having no evidence of His promises being made real—simply because He has proven that what He promised, He will perform. And because He has loved us in spite of ourselves—all that we are and all that we do—we continue to love Him unwaveringly, eternally. Or at least we should, but sometimes our humanity gets in the way.

Love and Love Alike

It is that same humanity that trips us up when it comes to loving those around us, yet Jesus says that all of the law hangs on those first two love commandments. How do the love instructions match up with the mighty ten? Well, it's safe to say that if we truly loved God, we wouldn't have any other gods beside Him, make idols of any kind, or misuse His Name in any way. It would be a joy to set aside one day a week of rest completely dedicated to Him. Now, if we truly love our parents, it would be easy to honor them, thereby reaping the reward of a long, fully satisfying life. If we truly love others, we would not become jealous and covet our neighbor's house, steal, or commit adultery. We would not become provoked and murder people (physically, with our

tongues, or in our minds). We would not rejoice in unrighteousness; therefore, we would not testify falsely against
our neighbor. We would be too busy believing the best
about those around us, rejoicing when something good
happened to anyone we knew. The Holy Spirit would have
to tell you that the person in front of you was lying because
you would always think the best of him and believe the
best of anyone who came your way.

I have a cousin who seems not to have one drop of
guile in her system. She always finds the good in people, no
matter how awful they have been to her or others. She
always gives their bad behavior a way of escape in her
rationale of the motive behind their actions. She always
believes the best and hopes the best for those around her.
Yet at the same time, she is extremely discerning. She can
see through a person in a hot second, and then she becomes
grieved because she wants that person to be better than he
or she is. Now I, with my little jaded self, have to admit my
envy of her state of heart. I would love to have a heart that
pure. It is hard for me to imagine her ever doing anything
deceitful because her heart is so full of love for everyone.
Though she clearly sees the ugliness of the world,
somehow she is able to rise above it all and not allow the
filth she sees to leave a residue on her spirit. She commits
those who insist on not being good into the hands of God.
"Oh, well, leave them to God," she says, trusting that God's
righteous judgment is better than any brand of retaliation
she could concoct.

Many feel that love will solve all of their problems and,
in one way, they are right. Love causes you to look past
many things that would otherwise be stumbling blocks.
However, rose-colored glasses don't fit into God's economy
of love. God's love sees things as they clearly are and offers
a solution. When He looked upon the face of the earth, He

said, "Ooh! Those people are full of sin; I've got to do something about that." He didn't pretend we were otherwise. He just set about a way of fixing our problem. Love is intimately involved and always in tune. Ever had someone walk up to you and ask, "Hi, how are you?" You say, "Terrible." And they respond, "That's good." They weren't really listening to you, were they? Weren't really hearing you or being sensitive to your spirit. Well, love isn't like that. Love listens. Perceives. Hears the unspoken. Weeps with those who weep. Rejoices with those who rejoice.

I recently purchased a new car and a friend of mine came over to check it out. He was so excited about my car, you would have thought it belonged to him. He finally said, "I am so happy for you! I love you so much that it just excites me when things are going well for you!" I thought that was so sweet. His joy was genuine over my blessing, and he truly rejoiced with me. It heightened the delight of sharing my good fortune with him as we raced off for a test drive together. Sharing the experience with my friend was a natural reaction to the joy he felt at my good fortune. He wasn't jealous, wondering why God had not blessed him with a new car, too. Instead he said that I had inspired him to believe in God for things. That's what love does. It spreads the wealth. Love makes the world an all-right place. Truly, love overcomes evil because who can stand against it? God in His infinite wisdom gave us the most delightful way of accentuating the positives and minimizing the negatives of life. It's no complex scientific formula or complicated tactical maneuver. It is the irrepressible gift of love.

On the Love Tip: Number Eight

If you're struggling in your love affair with God, try starting a romance journal. This is simply a book filled with all the love promises God has made to you in His Word.

Begin to seek Him during your quiet time, specifically asking Him to increase your love for Him. He knows what to do to warm your heart and draw you closer to Himself. Begin to add the unexpected blessings and sweet things that God makes obvious to you throughout your day. Get personal with God and what His Son Jesus did on your behalf. Personalize His crucifixion. See Jesus as a natural man, willing to do what He did for you purely out of His passionate love for you. Now write an engagement notice in your journal about your upcoming wedding to the Ultimate Bridegroom. He has gone to prepare a place for you and will return to take you to His heavenly Father's house. There He will introduce you to the heavenly community as His bride and bring you into a wedding feast that has been prepared for you. Until then, He anxiously awaits that day. Knowing that someone loves you and longs to bring you into such magnificence should fill your heart completely if you can press beyond the lofty God-in-the-sky concept and see Jesus as your Knight in Shining Armor coming on a white horse to carry you away. This is no fairy tale; this is the Word of God straight out of the book of Revelation. See, even our daydreams have spiritual origin. Now take the love that is beating in your heart for your heavenly fiancé and spread it among those who stand before you now. It should be easy because, after all, when love is in the air, no one can rain on your parade!

Love Note

I will betroth you to me for ever; yea, I will betroth
you to me in righteousness, and in justice, and in
lovingkindness, and in mercies.

9
Love Cover

The burly bodyguard stood blocking our entrance, arms folded, looking very determined. I decided this was about as much authority as this guy had ever experienced, and he was milking it for all it was worth. As he stood glowering down at us, I bristled under his glare, ready to serve up some choice words of intimidation as soon as I could think of something good. Shirley, on the other hand, was completely unruffled by the bodyguard's offensive demeanor, even as he huffed, "You can't get back there without a pass." Shirley simply smiled. "No problem," she sweetly answered. "I'm sure if you check the guest list, you'll find my name." She didn't bust a sweat as he gave her a suspicious sideways glance, as if sizing her up to see if she was capable of swishing past him while he looked down to check the clipboard he held in his hand like an army sergeant.

His eyebrow raised briefly after he spotted her name at the top of the list, then resumed its normal position to mask his admiration for her newfound importance in his eyes. She must know HIM intimately to be so prominently featured on the guest list. The difference in the bodyguard's manner was like night and day as he stepped aside and, with a sweeping motion, beckoned us into the hallowed backstage area. Shirley graciously acquiesced with no trace of snobbery, so intent was she on spotting HIM now that we were beyond the walls that had separated them up to this point. He appeared as if on cue to greet her with a warm embrace. This time the guard didn't bother to hide his surprise. From that moment on, all resistance to her presence vanished and no one dared to question her movements. She was free to come and go as she pleased with no hindrances or opposition; after all, she was with HIM.

This brought to mind an experience I had back in grade school. Coming to this country from the West Indies was a major adjustment at the tender age of seven. I came equipped with all the things it takes to make you a sitting target in the often cruel realm of elementary school—a heavy accent that no one could understand, an extremely skinny body, buck teeth (with a gap, no less!), and an I.Q. that surpassed my fellow miniature associates. This earned me the extraordinary opportunity to jump from first grade to third in a single bound and become the youngest among my peers. However, this feat was not admired or appreciated by those around me. While my teacher delighted in my acumen, I was despised by boys and girls alike as I was given the undesirable label of "teacher's pet." Needless to say, those were miserable days for me, days of loneliness and cruel treatment. The boys decided to nominate me as their punching bag while the girls simply sniffed past me in disdain. Who could save me from this heartless existence?

The only other oddball in the crowd, that's who. Ronald Alexander—we called him "Ronald Alick-a-zander"—towered above his classmates, so he, too, could relate to being different. He felt so sorry for me, bless his heart, that he decided to intervene in the midst of all this unfair treatment and become my protector. He proudly announced to everyone that I was his cousin; therefore, the next person who messed with me would be clobbered by him personally. Well, needless to say, that ended all the drama and I proceeded to survive the rest of the school year without further incident. It's all in who you know, they say, and that holds true in love and war. Especially when it comes to spiritual warfare.

Many struggle with wondering why they are having so little victory in their lives, why they have such problems taking dominion over their troubles. The solution to this is so simple that oftentimes we overlook it. When we draw close to God, He draws close to us, and the enemy has no choice but to flee. That's what a life covered by a solid love relationship with our Savior can do for us. Though God does allow the enemy to assault us from time to time for the sake of spiritual growth and maturity, the heart that is grounded in love is able to withstand the battle that rages around it. The prayer lines for deliverance would be drastically reduced if people could just tighten up their love relationship with God.

You are My friends, if you do what I command you.
—John 15:14 NASB, emphasis mine

Henceforth I call you not servants; for the servant knoweth not what his lord doeth: but I have called you

friends; for all things that I have heard of
My Father I have made known unto you.
          —John 15:15 NASB, emphasis mine

What then shall we then say to these things? If God
is *for us,* who is against *us?*
          —Romans 8:31 NASB, emphasis mine

The enemy of our souls cannot hang around if he knows that we are in cahoots with God Himself. The flip side of this is if he knows that your relationship with God is merely one of lip service and going through the motions of Christianity by rote, with no deep level of intimacy with the One you're serving, he merely laughs when you attempt to resist him. He has no power over a believer who is nestled in an intimate relationship with God. Consider the life of Job. Satan had to get permission from God to test him. Our effectiveness in spiritual warfare will be measured by our relationship with God. Think about how you would respond if you found out the cop pulling you over to the side of the road was only impersonating a policeman. Yes, he had on the uniform. Yes, he had all the right paraphernalia. But he had no real authority because he was not sanctioned by those who enforced the law to arrest you or give you a ticket. Why, you would just laugh and drive off, paying him no mind. So it is in the kingdom.

It's All in Who You Know

Remember those poor sons of Sceva in the book of Acts? Let me refresh your memory in order to prove my point.

And God was performing extraordinary miracles by
the hands of Paul, so that handkerchiefs or aprons

were even carried from his body to the sick, and the diseases left them and the evil spirits went out. But also some of the Jewish exorcists, who went from place to place, attempted to name over those who had the evil spirits the name of the Lord Jesus, saying, "I adjure you by Jesus whom Paul preaches." And seven sons of one Sceva, a Jewish chief priest, were doing this. And the evil spirit answered and said to them, "I recognize Jesus, and I know about Paul, but who are you?" And the man, in whom was the evil spirit, leaped on them and subdued all of them and over-powered them, so that they fled out of that house naked and wounded. And this became known to all, both Jews and Greeks, who lived in Ephesus; and fear fell upon them all and the name of the Lord Jesus was being magnified.

—Acts 19:11-17 NASB

Isn't that something? Can you imagine standing there rebuking the devil, and he says to you, "I know all about Jesus, but why should I listen to you? When was the last time you had a conversation with Him? And by the way, how are the two of you getting along?" Think about it. The devil knows your depth of relationship with Christ and, based on that, he may choose not to take you seriously. You see, he knows that if your relationship with Christ is not up to snuff, you are also struggling with believing His Word. He knows that you are not so sure if Jesus is backing you up or not. If you love Jesus, then you know who He is and you believe His Word because you know the One who sent Him. You are able to believe He now protects you and equips you with everything you need to be victorious against the enemy's attacks. But the opposite of that is one who is double-minded; that person cannot expect results (see James 1:7).

Sometimes we spend more time talking to the devil than we do to God. By the time we're done hurling spiritual commands at the enemy, we don't have enough energy to give glory to God because we're too busy worrying about which way the enemy is going to try to come next. We spend so much time strategizing about how to defeat him or to at least hold him at bay. But who died and gave the devil that much power? Certainly not Jesus! He died, rose, went down to Hades, snatched up the keys of hell, death, and the grave, released the captives who were bound, gave gifts to men, and revealed Himself to the disciples—all in three days' work. Shortly after, He ascended into heaven, took a deep breath, and sat down next to His Father to carry on his work. All in three days' work. And we struggle day after day wondering why the devil won't take his hands off of our affairs. Something isn't clicking properly here. Dare I say it is a relationship problem? Satan knows when we are out of sync with the Lover of Our Souls and takes full advantage of the love gap.

I heard a preacher once say, "Everyone is running around proclaiming they're taking back what the devil has stolen from them." His question to the audience that night was, "What if the devil doesn't have your stuff? What if God has it?" Speaking of things that make you go *hmmm!* Perhaps God isn't showing up as a defender because you've moved too far away from Him. Notice I said *you* moved. If you backtrack, I'm sure you'll find Him in the same spot you left Him in, waiting patiently for your return. Relationship with God is the most important spiritual weapon you can obtain before laying hold of all the others that Paul lists in the book of Ephesians. We cannot stand boldly defying the enemy if we have no confidence in our backup.

Friendship with God

When Moses was having a problem with the enemy, namely the Egyptians, God told him to go in His name to demand the Israelites' freedom. Moses went because God sent him. Sometimes I think we intentionally go wandering into territory we were told specifically not to enter, and when this happens we get in trouble. We are only sensitive in the spirit to know when to go or when to stay put, when to speak and when to be silent, if we are in fellowship with the Lord. It is in the quiet place with Him, in the mountaintop prayer experiences, that we are finally able to receive the instructions we need for overcoming. This is how true friendship operates. You sit and talk with a friend about your troubles. That friend then gives input into your situation that helps you to solve your dilemma. God wants to do the same for us. But sometimes, because we've learned a few Scriptures about our authority, we dash into the fray without consulting Him and then limp back afterwards worse for the wear, blaming God for our misfortune.

Moses received instructions every step of the way as he struggled with Pharaoh over the freedom of the Israelites. He and God were friends, co-conspirators in their quest to secure liberation for the children of Israel. They both wanted the same thing. Moses was not operating on his own personal agenda; he was determined to partner with God in His Kingdom plan. That's the other important factor at work here. When you are truly in love with God, you will be motivated, even in your battles, to keep His desires in mind. The motivation for the struggle will be different, thus ruling out a lot of selfish pursuits. Before you decide to fight for something, you will stop to ponder, "Is this something God wants for my life, or is this just something I have decided that I should have?" No longer will it be a matter of *your* rights. Instead, it will be about what God commissions. You've heard the saying, "When God gives the vision, He makes provision." It's true; He is more than happy to back up His own cause. Therefore, if you are in agreement with His cause, you can't help but have the victory. How do we know what He is interested in? By asking Him. Because of our love relationship, He responds with loving instruction.

Now, realize that the instructions will vary. He will either give us warfare strategies, as He gave to the kings and prophets of old, with very specific details, or He will say, "Step aside, this battle belongs to Me!" Naturally, I like the second choice the best. Sometimes He tells us to just praise Him and leave the fighting to Him as He did in the case of Jehoshaphat. You know, the story found in 2 Chronicles chapter twenty. The Moabites and Ammonites, along with some of the Meunites, came to make war against Jehoshaphat, King of Judah. As he bowed to seek the Lord and cry out for help, God sent a message.

...and he said, "Listen, all Judah and the inhabitants of Jerusalem and King Jehoshaphat: thus says the LORD to you, 'Do not fear or be dismayed because of this great multitude, for the battle is not yours but God's. Tomorrow go down against them. Behold, they will come up by the ascent of Ziz, and you will find them at the end of the valley in front of the wilderness of Jeruel. You need not fight in this battle; station yourselves, stand and see the salvation of the LORD on your behalf, O Judah and Jerusalem.' Do not fear or be dismayed; tomorrow go out to face them, for the LORD is with you."

—2 Chronicles 20:15-17 NASB

It is important to note that even when God is taking up the fight for us, we have a part to play. We must be in the correct posture to receive the victory. Think about it in terms of yourself. You will go out of your way to help someone who you know truly appreciates you and the help you offer. Jehoshaphat did something that ensured his victory. He did what the Lord told Him to do, but he also added a crucial ingredient to the mix—praise.

And they rose early in the morning and went out to the wilderness of Tekoa; and when they went out, Jehoshaphat stood and said, "Listen to me, O Judah and inhabitants of Jerusalem, put your trust in the LORD your God, and you will be established. Put your trust in His prophets and succeed." And when he had consulted with the people, he appointed those who sang to the LORD and those who praised Him in holy attire, as they went out before the army and said, "Give thanks to the LORD, for His lovingkindness is everlasting." When they began singing and praising, the LORD set ambushes against the sons of Ammon, Moab, and Mount Seir, who had come against Judah; so they were routed.

—2 Chronicles 20:20-22 NASB

Notice it was when they started singing and praising that the action began. They concentrated on the Lord and allowed Him to concentrate on what they couldn't handle. As we focus our hearts on Him, He rises to the occasion on our behalf. When our relationship with God is tight, the enemy is in trouble. God laughs at our enemies because He knows the fight is over before it has even begun, and that there is only one certain victor. No devil in his right mind would dare to mess with a child of God who keeps herself securely ensconced in the lap of her Savior. An angry God is not a pretty sight to behold; no demon would dare stir up His wrath. God does not take the distress of His beloved lightly.

You would be amazed at how involved God is in your protection. Recently I took a trip to Africa to deal with a family emergency. The spiritual warfare there was intense. On one hand I found myself struggling to pray. On the other hand, I had a tremendous sense of peace. So though I labored in prayer, I did not grow discouraged. I continued to press on, and marvelous breakthroughs came before I left Africa to return to the States. Upon my arrival back home, I was barraged with phone calls inquiring if I was all right. Each caller told me that the Lord had placed me on his or her heart and that the weight of me and my situation was so heavy that he or she was moved to pray on my behalf! As I began to share all that had occurred during the trip, we marveled at how much the Lord loves us. To think that He would move others to pray for me when I was having difficulty praying for myself brought me to tears as I reflected on His loving protection. I got a mental picture of Him holding the demons at bay, saying, "Oh, no! You are not going to mess with My baby. I love that girl. You've got to get past Me to get to her!" When you have a deep and abiding love relationship with the Lord, He stands against your enemies, whether you call or not. Oh, but when you call, He rises to the occasion and then some!

―――――――――――――♫―――――――――――――

I call upon the LORD, who is worthy to be praised, and I am saved from my enemies....In my distress I called upon the LORD, and cried to my God for help; He heard my voice out of His temple, and my cry for help before Him came into His ears. Then the earth

> *shook and quaked; and the foundations of the moun-*
> *tains were trembling and were shaken, because He*
> *was angry. Smoke went up out of His nostrils, and*
> *fire from His mouth devoured; coals were kindled by*
> *it. He bowed the heavens also, and came down with*
> *thick darkness under His feet. And He rode upon a*
> *cherub and flew; and He sped upon the wings of the*
> *wind. He made darkness His hiding place, His canopy*
> *around Him, darkness of waters, thick clouds of the*
> *skies. From the brightness before Him passed His*
> *thick clouds, hailstones and coals of fire. The* LORD
> *also thundered in the heavens, and the Most High*
> *uttered His voice, hailstones and coals of fire. He sent*
> *out His arrows, and scattered them, and lightning*
> *flashes in abundance, and routed them....They con-*
> *fronted me in the day of my calamity, but the* LORD
> *was my stay.*
> —Psalm 18:3,6-14,18 NASB

Get that picture in your mind the next time you feel overwhelmed by the onslaught of the enemy. God is faithful even when we are faithless. Ah, but to the soul that keeps its arms wrapped around His heart, He is an even fiercer defender.

David was a hopeless—or should I say, hopeful—romantic when it came to God. Because of his passionate love affair with the Lord, God showed up on David's behalf, in personal trial as well as when he stood before the nation. In the green pastures where David the shepherd boy continually sang love songs to the Lord, God kept him safe from the lion and the bear as well as from any unseen enemies. In the face of Goliath, God was literally the force behind David's arm as he wielded his slingshot against the giant. David was not a perfect man, but he *was* a man who loved God. He became indignant in the face of anyone or anything that threatened to insinuate that his God should not be taken seriously. And, like Moses when he pleaded for protection against the enemies who threatened the Israelites as they made their way to the promised land, David reminded God that He had a reputation to uphold before the nations. Victory is an important witness to those around us about the saving power of our Almighty God.

From the Beginning

It has always been God's desire for us to walk in dominion with Him as a reflection of His lordship in the heavens. Yet when Adam severed the love line with God in the garden with an act of willful disobedience, man has struggled to reinforce his authority ever since. When God came down to the garden to question Adam, He already had all the answers. He asked because He wanted Adam to know what his act had cost him. "Where are you, Adam?" was not a question about Adam's whereabouts as much as it was a psychological appeal to Adam to figure out the consequences of his behavior. "Do you know how your position in My kingdom has changed because of what you have done, Adam?" was what God meant. "Do you know what you forfeited when you chose to disobey Me?" Adam exchanged intimacy with God in order to become lord of his own destiny. Sin separates us from God. In his pursuit of the knowledge of good and evil, Adam lost valuable ground. He lost his authority status over his personal world, over the earth, and over the devil. The irony in all of this is that all he had to do was ask God what he wanted to know. He didn't have to eat a piece of fruit to find out anything! The lesson in this is that anything we choose to do apart from God is detrimental to our relationship with Him and to our own well-being. When we decide to do things on our own, we fight alone. And why would we want to do that? When we are in love, we want to include our beloved in everything we do.

Fellowship and intimacy with God insures our victory in life. The more victory we experience, the more reasons we have to praise Him. The more we praise Him, the more we are blessed, the more the enemy is put to flight, and the more we experience true Kingdom living. You see, it is all quite cyclical. One good turn begets another. Salvation is free, but victory comes with strings attached. And those strings should be wrapped around your heart.

On the Love Tip: In the Ninth Inning

I have a friend who is like a brother to me. We talk almost every day and have shared things with each other that no one else will ever know about. These are our secrets, which bind us together in a very special way. One day my friend said to me, "You know, I think I should give you a key to my home so that in case anything ever happened to me, you would be able to get in. Or in case I'm traveling and need you to check on something for me, you would be able to do it." I knew in that instant how much he trusted me. To give me access to his most treasured earthly possession, his home—the place that harbored all he held dear—was a deep thing.

Have you ever had trusted friends you were so close to that you trusted them with all of your belongings? You knew them so well that they were like a part of you. All that you had was also theirs. You withheld nothing from them. Well, Jesus has given us the keys to the kingdom (Matthew 16:19). He has given you access to all that He knows and all that He has. What a generous Lover He is! Begin to walk in the knowledge that you possess a real friendship—a love relationship with God. The potential of that friendship growing into something deep and abiding is up to you. Pause and reflect on God's goodness to you in the area of protection. Consider that every day you walk the streets of where you live and return home unscathed, while others face a different fate. You read about casualties in the newspapers and hear enough horrifying stories on the radio and television every day to realize by now that, if not for the grace of God and His abiding love for you, your situation could be drastically different. See God's protective hand operating in your life and give Him praise. And for those times when it seems as if the enemy is pressing in on every side, causing difficulties that seem too great to bear, pause and ponder God's love for you. Shut yourself away for a time of intimacy with Him. Await His instruction, and then face your enemy standing in the confidence that you are covered by the One who promises to fight on your behalf.

ℒove 𝒩ote

*Because you are so precious in my sight, and I have
loved you, I will give men for you, and people for
your life.*

10

The Language of Love

hirley licked the last envelope as if savoring a fine dessert, placed it on top of the stack, and patted the mound with great satisfaction. "There!" she said. Her work was finished. Earlier that afternoon I had discovered my friend at her desk deeply engrossed in her little project. Spread out before her were over thirty greeting cards, some beautiful, some funny. Carefully she selected a card one at a time. She would then gaze thoughtfully into space before writing a line inside of each one, signing off with her name written through a hand-drawn heart. Of course I surmised that all of these cards were for HIM.

"What's the special occasion?" I asked as Shirley turned up the volume on her CD player to fill the room with strains of "I Just Called to Say I Love You." "Huh?" she shouted over the music. "Is it his birthday or something?" I shouted back to her over the music she refused to lower. Gesturing at the stack of cards she was addressing, I waited for her to end her duet with Stevie Wonder and return the stereo to its regular volume. "Oh, that," she breathlessly answered. Then, taking note of my upraised brows, she continued, "No special occasion...just because." I suppressed a giggle by pressing my lips together tightly. Love had certainly done a number on my friend! "See, there's a card for every day of the month," Shirley explained. "Each one has a different reason I love him written inside. Oh! Check this one out. 'I love the way you listen to my heart and not just my words.'"

She leaned back in her chair, cradling the card against her breast as if reminiscing about some previous conversation between the two of them. "When I talk to HIM, he hangs on my every word as if what I was saying meant as much to HIM as it does to me. He is just so caring..." Her voice trailed off, lost in a reverie of tender moments, her eyes beginning to mist at the thought of how loved she felt. I thought that was just too precious. Her mood was so contagious that I could feel the tears threatening to fill my own eyes. Just as quickly, Shirley snapped out of her mood to exclaim, "Oh, I can't wait! He's gonna love this one. I can just see his face lighting up now." Then, sobering, she added, "You know, it's important to let people know unprompted how much you appreciate them."

As I gazed around Shirley's office filled with vases of the most magnificent roses I had ever seen—in addition to the breathtaking diamond heart pendant around her neck that he had given her—I wondered how hard it could be to give such a man words of appreciation. He was always giving her things, the most wonderful and original of presents. Even more, he was always there when she needed him. Shirley was truly a blessed woman. I was happy to see that she appreciated the gift he was to her life, just as he treated her as if she were a rare and precious jewel. The appreciation truly flowed both ways. This was an element of their relationship I enjoyed watching. They were so spontaneous with their adoration of one another. It seemed that they had found the secret for cultivating ongoing romance. As I got on the elevator, I thought to myself, *There's nothing like an unexpected word of praise and appreciation to set the heart in motion.*

Who doesn't feel all warm inside when someone calls to say, "I love you, just because"? We are so used to people having a hidden agenda that our response in those cases is usually a good-natured, "That's so sweet! Now what do you *really* want?" It seems that though we were created to be worshippers, the tendency to withhold praise has become a part of the fallen nature. We don't readily give praise for absolutely no reason—unless we are in love, that is. Think about the course of any good romance. In the beginning, when all is fresh and new, a couple is full of praise for one another. Any little thing becomes a reason to celebrate the specialness of each other.

From a new outfit to a good joke to just plain ole, "You make me feel so good when I'm with you," the compliments fly unfettered. But settle down into a good, stable marriage and the praise account dwindles sadly. Many men complain that their wives are not as amorous or ready to respond to their need for sexual intimacy as they were during courtship. The answer to this problem is simple. It's not just the demands of the day and the rigors of life that cause a woman to use the standard headache line; it is the lack of inspiration. Think about it. During the courtship stage, there were loving phone calls both morning and afternoon. By the time the evening rolled around, the couple was ready to burst, so great was their anticipation of seeing one another. It had been built up from the exchanges they'd had throughout the day. But now marriage has snuffed out the spontaneity and reduced romance to a dry duty. The passion is gone, no longer cultivated. It has been replaced by jobs, housecleaning, the kids.... No one notices the new outfit, the changed hairstyle, the smell of a nice cologne. Get the picture?

Many a wife has complained that her husband doesn't compliment her anymore. The husband's response is that no news is good news. Yet how can someone expect a response to nothing? A response is a reaction to some sort of stimulus. I believe God feels the same way. He seeks worshippers to worship Him. And His response to praise and worship is overwhelming! As I've mentioned earlier in the book, praise can set Him on the rampage against our enemies, but first I want to explore further how our praise and adoration cultivate intimacy with Him on a whole new level. If you are truly seeking to have a deeper love relationship with Him, this is the most important secret of all. Learning to praise God *just because* will work miracles in your life as well as deepen your ongoing relationship with your Savior.

Language of the Heart

Praise and worship is love talk, pure and simple. If you want to see the glory of God come down and surround you, just start lovin' on God. When couples are in love, they usually have their own pet names for one another. They pick a name that no one else uses in order to experience feelings of exclusivity. *Honey, Baby, Sweetheart* are names which let you know that these two people are close. Jesus taught us to pray and say, "Hallowed be Thy name." We know that Jesus is the Name above all other names, yet He has many titles. Depending on what you need from Him or how you feel about Him, you have an entire list of names to choose from—Jehovah Shalom, Jehovah, Rapha, Jehovah Jirah, Rose of Sharon, Lily of the Valley, Fairest of Ten Thousand...oh, don't get me started! I may not finish this book! So many marvelous names describe all that He is. Beginning to rehearse the names of the Lord is an exercise that will quicken your heart as you begin to take stock of His amazing attributes.

David meditated on who God was as he led his sheep to pasture. He called God his Rock, his Fortress, his Strong Tower. He praised God's capacity to provide in his life. He spoke of longing after God like a deer longs for a cool drink of water. Picture that! How soothing the presence of God must have been to David, a sweet and faithful companion in times of loneliness and isolation. A balm to his wounded soul. An invigorating source to draw from when his flesh was weary. A comforter in times of deep disappointment. He had a long list of names for God that he utilized in psalms to Him, describing all that his Lord was to his seeking heart. As we continue to lose ourselves in the attributes of the Lover of Our Souls, we are overcome with His presence and true intimacy becomes a reality.

I recall a specific instance of this as I was experiencing a particularly distressing hardship in my life. I determined not to allow my circumstances to overwhelm me. Instead, I was going to purpose in my heart to praise the Lord, even though I truly did not feel like talking to Him, much less praising Him. However, I knew the secret to my breakthrough was in pressing past the grudge that I was bearing against God for allowing me to experience such difficulty. I simply needed to begin to talk it out. But first I needed to reignite our relationship. So I shut myself in, determined to retrace my steps to the place where our love relationship began. I turned off the phone and tuned out the world. This was going to be a time deliberately set aside just for me and God.

I began with all of my favorite worship songs—"His Name Is Wonderful"; "I Love You, Lord"; "There's Just Something About That Name"; "When I Look into Your Holiness." The more I sang, the more praises came to my mind. It was as if a fountain had opened up in my soul. What started as me sitting in a chair in a relaxed position crescendoed to me standing tall with my arms raised heavenward. And when I could think of no more songs to sing, I praised Him for all that He had done, for who He was, for all of His wonderful characteristics, for past blessings and evidences of His love for me. When I could say no more, all I could do was weep, so overcome was I with His presence and His glory. I sensed Him filling the room with His magnificence, surrounding me with His heart. I felt closer to Him than ever before in that moment. And then came the question resounding in my spirit in the midst of the stillness: "What do you want, My love?" I knew it was Him, and I felt that I would receive whatever I asked for in that moment; yet I could think of nothing. Nothing at all! At that moment my car was in the shop and I had no money to get it out. There was a five-day eviction notice under my door, and I had no money to pay the rent. My refrigerator was empty, and I had no money to buy food. Still, I could think of nothing that I needed, so caught up was I in His presence. Nothing else seemed important. I was distracted from all the unpleasantries of life. He was all that I could see, all that I longed for.

"I just want more of You," was all I could manage between my tears and my praise. Sensing His presence, I felt the reality of Him surrounding me like a magnet pulling me to bow down and worship. I worshiped as I had never worshipped before. And when His glory finally lifted and my praises subsided, new hope was birthed in my heart. He was real, His love for me was more real than I had ever imagined. He cared about me and my circumstances; He was on my side. Regardless of what my eyes presently saw—the needs, the unpaid bills, the empty cupboards—God was present and working in my life. Surely goodness and mercy would follow me. I had His promise.

This was when I discovered that worship and faith were intricately woven together to form the strength and fiber of my inner man. Praise and worship brought me into His presence, but His presence reaffirmed our intimacy. It was that sense of intimacy which caused me to dare to believe in what I termed the impossible. Shortly after this occurrence, I experienced a major breakthrough in my life and situation. My old employer called me back to work with the offer of an unbelievable raise, and my life changed drastically for the better. It was as if the tap of blessings had been released from heaven itself and I was swimming in the overflow.

The Sacrifice of Love

What is it about praise that opens the way for blessings and victory to flow into our lives? What really happens when we praise God? Praise is the recalibration of our spirit. It puts everything back in the right position. Praise and worship are the ultimate surrender. They say, "Yes, God, You truly are Lord." If there was ever any question about it, it is settled when we enter into praise and worship and all attention turns to Him. The closer we get to Him, the smaller our troubles become.

I recall speaking at a conference last year when, during the afternoon session, we were all given slips of paper and instructed to write down our concerns and cares on them. These troublesome issues were then rolled up and inserted inside of balloons that had been filled with helium. Next we went outdoors and prayed and sang songs of praise before the Lord as we released our balloons. We gazed in amazement as the balloons floated higher and higher, finally disappearing completely into the clouds. I turned to the ladies who now stood weeping, the light of hope filling their faces, and said, "Isn't it amazing that when we hold on to our problems they seem so huge, but the moment we give them to God and totally let go, they are completely diminished? The farther out of our reach they get and the closer they travel to God, the smaller they become. They are insignificant in comparison to His glory." As His glory surrounds us, He becomes more real to us. It is this feeling of togetherness with Him that leads us to a greater place of obedience and faith. These are the dynamic duo for receiving a blessing.

Praise and worship are the deepest forms of intimacy you can experience with Christ. When you truly press past yourself into the Holy of Holies within your spirit, you return to the garden in a sense. Once again, man or woman becomes naked and unashamed in the presence of a Holy God. It is rendering yourself completely vulnerable, accessible to the touch of God. It is the place of offering yourself as a living sacrifice. Opening your hands and confessing that they are empty. Extending your arms and proclaiming them helpless without Him. Submitting your body to be a vessel used only for the Master's purposes. Praise and worship are analogous of the natural act of sexual intercourse in that surrender is involved. Small wonder the heathen included sex in their worship rites to pagan gods. They understood the significance of this display of surrender. It was their way of offering their bodies as living sacrifices to their gods.

We, too, are asked to render our bodies as living sacrifices unto God.

I urge you therefore brethren, by the mercies of God, to present your bodies a living and holy sacrifice, acceptable to God, which is your spiritual service of worship.
—Romans 12:1 NASB, emphasis mine

God requires the same cleansing of our hearts, hands, and bodies as He did of the priests who were called to serve Him in the Holy of Holies. The same passing through the blood (significant of the virginal passage typified through purification by the blood of Jesus) and the same clearing away of all offenses applies. Let's face it. None of us feels very amorous toward a partner who has offended us. God now invites us all individually, represented by one High Priest only (Jesus Himself), to enter into His presence bringing our own worship and sacrifices of praise, to undress ourselves per se of all that keeps us from drawing closer to Him, and to become like Him as we see Him face to face, heart to heart, spirit to spirit, joining to and becoming one with Him. It's like a relationship between two married people. Even as a husband and wife become one physically, their souls connect as they express their love for one another.

So how can we render our bodies as sacrifices to God if our hearts are not in cooperation with our members? This is where the cheerful giving of one's self comes in to play. As our hearts are filled with praise for the One who loves us most, we will find our bodies lining up in the worshipful posture of obedience. Obedience is a major portion of what

God calls worshipping in spirit and in truth. The spirit part resides in the heart, the will, or seat of decision-making and emotions. But the truth part is when your body lines up with what your heart believes. You begin showing yourself true to God by walking it out before Him. Many pray to God without ever considering whom they are truly talking to. They talk *at* a Holy God and await His response—not really His response to them, but to the situation they want fixed. This does not help in developing a relationship or nurturing intimacy. It is the gazing into His eyes, feeling His heart, recognizing and rehearsing His attributes, that draw us into His arms. Perhaps David said it best.

Bless the LORD, O my soul; and all that is within me, bless His holy name. Bless the LORD, O my soul, and forget none of His benefits.
—Psalm 103:1,2 NASB

Oh give thanks to the LORD, call upon His name; make known His deeds among the peoples. Sing to Him, sing praises to Him; speak of all His wonders. Glory in His holy name; Let the heart of those who seek the LORD be glad. Seek the LORD and His strength; seek His face continually.
—Psalm 105:1-4 NASB

You might say to me, "Michelle, I don't always feel like praising the Lord. And I still don't understand how to reach that place of praising Him with complete abandon. I feel silly sitting in a room waiting for God to show up." Let me help you out with this. The first thing you must understand is that praise and worship involve the will as well as the emotions. This is why David seemed to be giving instruction to himself so many times in the psalms. People laugh at me when they catch me talking to myself. This is my way of focusing when I feel scattered. I will stop in the middle of the chaos and say to myself, "Okay, Michelle, you are supposed to be looking for *x, y,* or *z.* You can come back to this; this is off the beaten path." Remember that God called everything into existence through the spoken Word. As believers, we now share this amazing ability with Him. Sometimes we need to talk to ourselves and say, "Self, though I don't feel like it, yet will I praise the Lord!"

Why art thou cast down, O my soul? and why art thou disquieted in me? hope thou in God: for I shall yet praise *him for the help of his countenance.*
—Psalm 42:5 KJV, emphasis mine

Why art thou cast down, O my soul? and why art thou disquieted within me? hope thou in God: for I shall yet praise *him, who is the health of my countenance, and my God.*
—Psalm 42:11 KJV, emphasis mine

Why art thou cast down, O my soul? and why art thou disquieted within me? hope in God: for I shall yet praise *him, who is the health of my countenance, and my God.*
—Psalm 43:5 KJV, emphasis mine

But I will hope continually, and will yet praise *thee more and more.*
—Psalm 71:14 KJV, emphasis mine

Yes, praise is like exercise. The more you do it, the more you will want to do it. It was this exercise that strengthened David to overcome the lion, the bear, and eventually Goliath. He was intimate with God and arose to defend His name in the face of a giant unbeliever. What fueled his indignation at Goliath, this overgrown bully? Not the fact that he threatened the armies of Israel, but rather that he showed no respect toward God and cursed David by his pagan gods. As if they had more power than the God David knew! When we are in love and are well acquainted with the goodness of our lover's ways, there is no way we will allow anyone else to insult him. No one can say anything negative about the one we praise. It was love that gave David the passion he needed to get the victory. It was the remembrance of romantic times spent with his Savior, the assurance of their intimacy, the knowledge of how wonderful God was. He knew of His faithfulness and friendship. He knew the Lover of His Soul was by his side.

This is the path to the deepest knowledge of God's heart that you can have. The more you find His heart revealed to you through the Scriptures, the more you can begin to pause and consider every line. As you internalize it, personalize it, and then rehearse it again in praise, something revolutionary will happen. As you read, God will come to life on those pages. He will come alive in your heart. There is an intangible in this type of intimacy with God that will be hard to vocalize and hard to explain, yet you will know when you arrive at this level. Yes, you will know, that you know, that you know. It will bubble up on the inside of you as you walk down the street. You will be overwhelmed by thoughts of His love at the most unusual moments. You will find yourself praising Him without thinking about it. Such praise will become a part of you, overflowing in the midst of the ordinary and not-so-ordinary instances of life. It will bring a smile to your face in unexpected moments and cause others to wonder about the change in your countenance.

...And though you have not seen Him, you love Him, and though you do not see Him now, but believe in Him, you greatly rejoice with joy inexpressible and full of glory.

—1 Peter 1:8 NASB

Such is love. It's hard to explain, and yet it is what it is. Praise refills the fountain of your soul to overflowing so that your spirit might refresh others. So praise. Not just for God's sake, but for your own heart's sake. For the sake of others around you. Because praise is the greatest way to spread the love.

On the Love Tip: Tenth in Line

If we work from the premise that praise sets the atmosphere for the glory of God to fill our lives, we must realize that we are literally talking about putting God in the mood to show up in our personal world. As the saying goes, "When the praises go up, the blessings come down." And it is true. This is the secret to being overtaken with gifts and presents from God. You know, what we term blessings and miracles.

So how to go about getting in the mood for putting God in the mood? Let's copy Shirley. Purpose to write God little love notes or present Him with a daily card for thirty days telling Him how much you love Him and why. Now, you must come up with a new reason for loving Him every day, so be original here. This will also get you past your four favorite catch phrases for Him and make you expand the breadth of your experiences with Him. As you begin to discover Him in the little things in your life, you will become aware of how concerned He is with every little detail of your life. That's when the fire in your own heart will burn brighter than ever before and the true romance will begin.

Love Note

*I long to dwell in your heart through faith so that
you may be rooted and grounded in my love and be
able to comprehend with all the saints the breadth
and length and height and depth of my love for you
that surpasses knowledge. For my lovingkindness
toward you reaches to the heavens.*

11

Recapturing the Passion

hirley dabbed one last drop of her favorite perfume behind her ears and gave herself a final look of approval as she threw her stole over her shoulders. "And where are we off to this evening?" I inquired. "He said it was a surprise," she giggled. "Did he get a promotion or something?" I queried. I was quite curious about this date 'cause girl-friend was dressed to the nines, okay? "Nooo...it's our anniversary!" Shirley preened. "Ahh, I see!" I replied. "And which one is this?" I humored her. "It was exactly twelve months ago on this very day that we met. At exactly one o'clock. That's why we always have lunch together at one o'clock on the third of every month, and we always spend a special evening together," she explained.

"How long do you plan to keep this up?" I asked. "This could be an expensive habit." Shirley looked at me for a moment, as if measuring how to phrase her response. Slowly and seriously, as if to emphasize every word, she said, "It could be expensive *not* to indulge in this habit. When people begin to take one another for granted, romance dies quickly." On that note, she went back to preparing for her special time with HIM.

I left Shirley setting the mood for a romantic evening with strains of "The First Time Ever I Saw Your Face" floating in the air behind me and the scent of sandalwood candles blending with the smell of the fresh flowers that filled her apartment. Flowers sent by—who else?—HIM.

How insightful of my friend to note the dangers of letting love just run its course. She had a serious point. Love is like a tender plant. It has to be nurtured in order to grow. Left to its own devices, with no care, no water, and no light, it eventually withers and dies. It is imperative that we do whatever it takes to keep love alive.

Why is it essential that we keep our love affair with God fresh? When God addressed the church at Ephesus in the second chapter of Revelation, His charge to them was to return to their first love. If they did not, He would remove their lampstands from their place. As we search the Scriptures, we see that the lampstands stood before the consecrated bread in the holy place in the presence of the Lord, reflecting His light. What were the lampstands all about? We know that in the Word, lamps represent the very presence of God and the light that His Word brings.

Thy word is a lamp *to my* feet *and a light to my path.*
—Psalm 119:105 NASB, emphasis mine

The city does not need the sun or the moon to shine on it, for the glory of God gives it light, and the Lamb is its lamp.
—Revelation 21:23 NIV, emphasis mine

Which brings us back full circle to the Lord, because Jesus is the Word in the flesh. In Revelation the lampstands symbolize the churches established by God. The churches were now supposed to reflect the presence of God, making His love, His wisdom, and His power real to the world. If they had no light, this would be impossible.

For with you is the fountain of life; in your light we see light.
—Psalm 36:9 NIV, emphasis mine

You are the light of the world. A city on a hill cannot be hidden. Neither do people light a lamp and put it under a bowl. Instead they put it on its stand, and it gives light to everyone in the house. In the same way, let your light shine before men, that they may see your good deeds and praise your Father in heaven.
—Matthew 5:14-16 NIV

No one lights a lamp and puts it in a place where it will be hidden, or under a bowl. Instead he puts it on its stand, so that those who come in may see the light. Your eye is the lamp of your body. When your eyes are good, your whole body also is full of light. But when they are bad, your body also is full of darkness.
—Luke 11:33,34 NIV

The eye is the lamp *of the body. If your eyes are good,*
your whole body will be full of light.
—Matthew 6:22 NIV, emphasis mine

See *to it, then, that the* light *within you is not dark-*
ness. Therefore, if your whole body is full of light, and
no part of it dark, it will be completely lighted, as
when the light of a lamp shines on you.
—Luke 11:35,36 NIV, emphasis mine

If we don't view the rudiments of life and the world
around us through the eyes of God and His perspective in
accordance with His Word, we are in darkness. And it is
impossible to reflect what we do not truly see. When the
eyes of our understanding are darkened, our life will
expose our lack of spiritual understanding and show that
we are at odds with God. How do we leave the light and
stumble into such a miserable place? It's simple. Darkness
fills a soul that turns from God in pursuit of other loves.
Even in the midst of religious activity, the heart can stray
from the hearth of His love and grow cold. If we, individually or corporately, do not nurture our love relationship
with God, we will fail to have the open communication we
need with Him in order to walk in the light. We will be left
to grope in the darkness of our own bad decisions, stumbling over failure and mishap after mishap. Victory eludes
those who wander from the presence of God. This makes us
powerless witnesses to the rest of the world. They see our
state of chaos and find no reason to embrace the Christ we
attempt to introduce to them. The growing disdain the
world has for Christians should give us cause to admit that

we are on the threshold of seeing God's warning to the Ephesian church come to light. And all of this is happening because of a lack of love—for God and for one another.

Try to Remember

James Ingram sang the question all lovers ask: "How do you keep the music playing?" If this is a difficult question to answer when you're involved with someone you can see, how much more difficult is it to keep the flame of passion burning bright toward a God we cannot see? The Ephesian church was no stranger to the concept that love should be the motivating factor fueling all that one did for God. This was stressed over and over again in Paul's words to them. Those who had been ardent in their pursuit of idols and Greek deities were now just as devoted to the pursuit of godly living. But now their heart involvement was required along with their intellectual commitment.

And I pray that you, being rooted and established in love, may have power, together with all the saints, to grasp how wide and long and high and deep is the love of Christ, and to know this love that surpasses knowledge—that you may be filled to the measure of all the fullness of God.
    —Ephesians 3:17-19 NIV, emphasis mine

Be completely humble and gentle; be patient, bearing with one another in love.
    —Ephesians 4:2 NIV, emphasis mine

Instead, speaking the truth in love, we will in all things grow up into him who is the Head, that is,

Christ. From him the whole body, joined and held together by every supporting ligament, grows and builds itself up in love, *as each part does its work.*
—Ephesians 4:15, 6 NIV, emphasis mine

...and live a life of love, *just as Christ loved us and gave himself up for us as a fragrant offering and sacrifice to God.*
—Ephesians 5:2 NIV, emphasis mine

———————————————*m*———————————————

It seemed that the Ephesians were faithful in Christian duty, but "religious." When they discovered Jesus Christ, they merely transferred their ritualistic behavior from the false gods they had served to religious devotion to the one and only True God. They were used to the discipline of religion. Paul made note to compliment them for their faithful striving to be obedient to God, but he redirected their motivations back to a relational place. He stressed that their acts of righteousness could not be considered payment for the free gift of salvation. They had lived for so long under the duties of appeasing false gods to earn invisible blessings that it was now difficult for them to grasp the concept of an almighty God giving free gifts just because. Just because He loved them! So they put their noses to the ritualistic grindstone and ground away. Does this sound like anyone you know?

Even God could find almost no fault with the Ephesian church. They didn't tolerate evil. They took the time to be discerning of leaders who attempted to rise up in their midst. He had no criticisms for the church board, the basic governmental structure, or practices of the church body. He only had one complaint. They were so busy being good that they forgot *why* they were being good! They had forgotten they were having a *relationship* with Him. It was affecting how they treated others. They had ceased to walk in love, so caught up were they in being theologically correct. They were spiritually on but relationally off. And God wasn't feeling very loved by them. What was the problem? They had forgotten what Paul had told them.

Remember when Jesus kept asking Peter if Peter loved Him? Consider what Jesus asked for as proof of that love.

This was now the third time Jesus appeared to his disciples after he was raised from the dead. When they had finished eating, Jesus said to Simon Peter, "Simon son of John, do you truly love me more than these?" "Yes, Lord," he said, "you know that I love you." Jesus said, "Feed my lambs." Again Jesus said, "Simon son of John, do you truly love me?" He answered, "Yes, Lord, you know that I love you." Jesus said, "Take care of my sheep." The third time he said to him, "Simon son of John, do you love me?" Peter was hurt because Jesus asked him the third time, "Do you love me?" He said, "Lord, you know all things; you know that I love you." Jesus said, "Feed my sheep."

—John 21:14-17 NIV

Just think! Peter was the one who understood who Jesus was. Jesus had told him he had received divine insight into His identity. He told Peter that he had been given the foundational key to the establishment of the church. No matter how much insight Peter had, no matter how much zeal he had concerning Christ, Jesus was not moved by religious fervor or theological accuracy. He asked Peter to feed His sheep. Not *beat* the sheep; *feed* them—nurture and care for them. In other words, Jesus was saying, "I am on My way out of here. If you truly love Me, you will treat My lambs the way you would treat Me if I were still with you. If you can't do that, then I know that our romance has gotten off-track and you don't love Me as you once did." Whoa! The straight-up truth—down and dirty.

There is a welcome song some churches sing to their visitors that goes something like, "The Jesus in me loves the Jesus in you, that's so easy to do." Well, it should be easy, but what if the love tank for Jesus is running close to empty? That doesn't leave too many drops of love for anyone else, does it? Could it be that the Ephesian church was running a buttoned-up institution but wasn't being very nice to others? Could it be that they were being unpleasant and judgmental? Could it be that their love for God and patience with the shortcomings of others—their compassion for the brethren—had gone out the window as they went about their business, storing up brownie points for the kingdom? As God appealed to the Ephesian church to return to their first love, He gave them some solid hints to help them reignite their love relationship with Him. I think these hints can help us, as well.

Remember the height from which you have fallen! Repent and do the things you did at first. If you do not repent, I will come to you and remove your lampstand from its place.

—Revelations 2:5 NIV, emphasis mine

Do you remember the euphoria you felt when salvation was brand-new? How relieved you were to be forgiven by God? Love and gratitude bubbled up in your heart. The testimony of His deliverance was ever fresh on your lips. You were on a natural, spiritual high. Every day was a day to praise the Lord because the recollection of where He had brought you from was still fresh in your memory. Every sermon seemed to apply to you as you soaked up the instructions to maintaining your newfound freedom. Every worship song moved your heart because you could second the motion of the psalmists. Your eyes sparkled. You smiled a lot. You felt as if you were going to burst, so filled was your heart with love for your newfound Savior. People noticed a difference in your countenance and wanted to know what was new with you. They wanted what you had. You literally radiated peace and joy. You had the faith to move mountains and take hold of miracles. You could see the invisible. You could feel the intangible. Your confidence in the Lover of Your Soul was so profound that others asked you to pray for them, too. Do you remember?

Knowing God was exciting then. Every day was a new opportunity to see His faithfulness in a whole new way. You took careful note of miracles in your life, both great and small. When you met other Christians, you bonded with them big-time. You were so excited to meet a new friend who shared the same love you did for the Lord. But somewhere along the way things changed. Maybe people began to comment that you had become a bit too fanatical about your faith. So you made adjustments. Vigor gave way to dry habits. And then maybe someone in church wounded you. You witnessed things happening in ministry that rocked your faith. You suffered disappointments in your life. God didn't show up the way you thought He should in the midst of your situation. Protecting your heart took the place of passion. Religion took the place of relationship. When you couldn't see God's hand in your life, you stopped trusting His heart toward you. If this has happened to you, it's time to take stock of where you are, how far you've drifted, and take the second step God advises—repent.

Love Means You Never Have to Say You're Sorry?

Now let's talk about repenting for a minute since this is the second hint God offers to help us restir the fires of passion. Once we apologize to God for neglecting Him, we can't return to our same old mode of behavior. To truly repent means that we have an authentic change of heart. We do not return to business as usual. How do we have a change of heart? We see our behavior and attitudes as God sees them. This is the essence of confession—not admitting what we've done from *our* vantage point, but rather calling it as *God* sees it. While we might attribute our prayerlessness to being distracted by worldly cares, guess what God would call it? Yup, you're right—prayerlessness. While we might call making other things more important than God a case of misplaced priorities, God calls it idolatry, plain and simple. As we confess to Him that we have not been cultivating our relationship with Him the way we ought to and we ask Him to help us draw closer to Him, He rises to the occasion. All that is required is our cooperation, which brings me to the last thing that God advises. He wants us to revisit our first attitudes and behaviors and do what we did then.

Starting All Over Again

Revisit how it was when you first came to the Lord. Renew your vows to Him. Refresh your love for the Word of God. Begin to read the Bible as if you have never read it before. Try a different translation and get a new perspective of the big picture, or do a word study on a subject that concerns you. Recall how you drank in every sermon and conversation about this newfound Savior. Find some good Bible teachers you enjoy and order their tapes. Play them on the way to work in your car, or listen to them as you do your chores around the house. Renew your hunger for God, your thirst for any information or fellowship that would bring you closer to Him. Begin to feed your spirit more than your flesh. Refresh your enthusiasm for going to the house of the Lord. Volunteer for something that you are passionate about. If there is a ministry you feel is missing at your church, perhaps you should be the one to get it started. Remember the overwhelming desire you had to tell everyone you knew about your salvation experience. Begin to witness to others again. As you renew your mind by feeding your spirit the way you did as a new believer, your love life with God will be transformed.

Ask God to show you when and why the fire cooled and why your heart went from a high boil to a quiet simmer. Ask Him to help you locate when your passion was replaced by more conventional modes of worship and behavior that lacked the spontaneity and excitement of before. And then ask Him to relight the fire.

Looking Back

I recall how I used to fast regularly once a week. Back then, I also began every year with a forty-day fast. If a matter was pressing in my prayer life, I would commit to at least a seven-day fast until I felt that thing break apart in the spirit. Like I said, that's the way I started off. Somewhere along the way it became more difficult to commit to regular fasting. I had to pray and ask God to help me get back on track.

Retracing my steps back in time to when I first met God made me see how far I had fallen away from the things I used to do to cultivate our relationship. I kept a Bible in my desk at work. Every break I got, my nose was buried in the pages. I couldn't wait to get home at night to talk with my friend Harry, who was attending theological school. I would then press him with questions about all the things I had read throughout the day that I didn't understand. Every opportunity to hear about God was an occasion to be attended. Oh, how I loved Him! He was all I talked about. My thoughts were filled with Him. Just when I lost that lovin' feelin', I'm not sure. But I had to admit that God was right. I needed to repent of my lack of attention toward Him.

Moving On

This is not the time to fall into self-condemnation or get so fixated on the way we were that we are unable to move forward. Dwelling on the past and comparing today or tomorrow with yesterday can be paralyzing, as Lot's wife found out.

But Lot's wife looked back, and she became a pillar *of* salt.

—Genesis 19:26 NIV, emphasis mine

God's ultimate desire is that we move from glory to glory with Him. He is interested in forward motion.

And we, who with unveiled faces all reflect the Lord's glory, *are being transformed into his likeness with ever-increasing* glory, *which comes* from *the Lord, who is the Spirit.*

—2 Corinthians 3:18 NIV, emphasis mine

Don't fight the feeling. Go with the flow. Let your heart go where His Spirit takes you. Dare to launch into the deep with the only One who will never disappoint, reject, or forsake you. It is His love and His love alone that feeds all other loves, but He must be first.

On the Love Tip: In the Eleventh Hour

The Lord is not interested in coasting at the same level with us. He is not interested in staying in a stale marriage or an uneventful love relationship. And let's face it, neither are you. In that case, you have the perfect love partner. He is passionate. He has more than a mild interest in you. He intensely longs after you all the time. And you need to be able to say "back at-cha." So become a creative lover. Just think about how you feel when any routine in your life becomes too predictable. Boredom sets in, doesn't it? So shake up your schedule a little. Don't just pray in the morning. Call Him up in the middle of the day. Talk to Him about that driver who almost sideswiped you. Invite Him to go to lunch with you. Make a date to tell Him how much you love Him just because. You won't find a better Lover than Him, you know.

Here's a tip to help get you started. Recently I attended a very special wedding. My friends Frank and P.B. "Bunny" Wilson were renewing their wedding vows. Oh, the look of love in their eyes! You see, in preparation for this day, they'd had plenty of time to think back over all the things they had come through together. How blessed they were to have one another and still be in love after all this time. No, let me rephrase that. How blessed they were to have one another and to be *more* in love now than when they'd started off. They had grown together, developing a beautiful oneness that was apparent to everyone who met them. As Bunny entered the church on that special day, a collective gasp came from the audience. She was absolutely breathtaking. It was difficult to decide where to let your eyes linger. Perhaps on her exquisite white dress with its incredible lace overcoat. Or maybe on her face, which was so beautiful! She was literally glowing. Her eyes were alive with words intended only for her beloved. You could almost feel the catch in Frank's throat as he beheld her in that moment.

And then the music started. On this special day, Frank sang a song he had written especially for his lovely wife as she walked down the aisle. There wasn't a dry eye in the house as he passionately serenaded her, "I love you from a place within myself. Untravelled by those worn cliches. A very private street inspired and conceived to bring a deep and quiet love from me to you. Precious like a stone collector buys. Or a picture painted for the Master's eye. These feelings that I keep locked away inside, they're just for you...." Whew! I thought Bunny was going to lose it. Shoot, I thought *I* was going to lose it! Now, that's some love! Don't you want a man in your life who sings a song of love to you like that? Well you have One! His name is Jesus and His banner over you is love. So why not have your own ceremony and renew your commitment to Him? Remember. Repent. Renew. And find your way back to your first love.

Love Note

Though the mountains shall depart, and the hills will be removed, my kindness and love will never depart from you. Neither will my covenant of peace we share between us be removed.

12

The Greatest of These...

hirley's face radiated the peace and tranquility of a bride who was ready in every way. Today was the day she was to marry HIM. Her dress was pure white, simply elegant, undisturbed by any unnecessary adornment. Her headpiece, though exquisite, was not distracting. Truly, I had a vision of how it must look when God's train filled the temple as yards and yards of netting were arranged behind Shirley, giving the semblance of her rising from the clouds. Her neck was like an elegant tower rising from the very simple thread of platinum, more expensive and durable than even gold, that held the ever-present diamond heart that he had given her. Today the diamond blazed against her skin as if it were illuminated from within. The only thing more luminous were her eyes. They glowed with the light of love in her flawless face. And she wore the diamond earrings that he had given to her on this, her wedding day, to seal the covenant of love he had written to her in beautiful script on parchment just that afternoon. Her excitement gave all the color she needed to her cheeks and temples. Her skin was like burnished bronze with a dewy patina from the warmth of the day. Her lips were soft with just the right touch of natural tint. Naturally perfect from head to toe, she lowered her veil and waited for the music that would herald her entrance.

As strains of "Here Comes the Bride" filled the sanctuary and everyone rose to receive the woman now slowly beginning her ascent up the aisle, I turned to view the groom's face. I must admit that I usually ignore the groom at weddings; once he takes his position at the foot of the altar, I turn to examine the bride in all her adornment. But today I wanted to see if he truly appreciated what he was getting. Appreciation sounded trite in light of what I witnessed on his face. It could be compared only to a glorious sunrise. Just as the sky changed colors when the sun crept higher in the firmament, the depth of his emotion became more apparent the closer toward him Shirley came. *Oh, how he loves her,* I thought. It could not be denied. He trembled as he waited to take her hand, so great was his anticipation of finally becoming one with her. As Shirley's father released her into the care of her waiting husband-to-be, the look between them could have set the world on fire. It was as if everyone present was holding his or her breath, not daring to infringe on this moment of intimate communication between them by making the slightest of sounds. Yes, everyone was in agreement that truly they could hold their peace and allow these two lovers to complete their vows.

The Heart of the Bridegroom

Long after the festivities had ended and the couple had headed off for their honeymoon, I could not get HIM off my mind. I don't think I had ever seen a man's face filled with so much love before. Perhaps I had never even imagined love like that! I wondered to myself how it would feel to have someone look at me in that way. *"Don't you know?"* the Holy Spirit whispered to me. *"I'm the One who loves you so much, I've even counted every strand of hair on your head, so intently do I gaze upon you. I am waiting and anticipating our wedding day, too. I have been longing to become one with you since before eternity began, and still I wait."* This brought a smile to my face. Of course! I *do* know how it feels to be loved in that way! What a feeling of security it is to be in love with the One who loves me most. It causes me to relax in the care of my Savior with no fear of what the future may bring. I realized that this was why Shirley could be so peaceful on her wedding day, so free from trepidation. She knew she was loved. She knew she had a good man. Her knowledge flavored her attitude and response toward all of her dealings with HIM.

And so it is with God. I have spent years befuddled at why some people seem to flourish in their relationship with God while others seem to be in a perpetual stalemate. Though those who were stuck said they loved the Lord, they seemed to be more negative, more suspicious of God's motives, and less trusting. This reminded me of a parable Jesus shared with the disciples about the talents. There are some key things to look at in this section of Scripture.

Again, it will be like a man going on a journey, who called his servants and entrusted his property to them. To one he gave five talents of money, to another two talents, and to another one talent, each according to his ability.... After a long time the master of those servants returned and settled accounts with them. The man who had received the five talents brought the other five. "Master," he said, "you entrusted me with five talents. See, I have gained five more." His master replied, "Well done, good and faithful servant! You have been faithful with a few things; I will put you in charge of many things. Come and share your master's happiness!" The man with the two talents also came. "Master," he said, "you entrusted me with two talents; see, I have gained two more." His master replied, "Well done, good and faithful servant! You have been faithful with a few things; I will put you in charge of many things. Come and share your master's happiness!" Then the man who had received the one talent came. "Master," he said, "I knew that you are a hard man, harvesting where you have not sown and gathering where you have not scattered seed. So I was afraid and went out and hid your talent in the ground. See, here is what belongs to you." His master replied, "You wicked, lazy servant! So you knew that I harvest where I have not sown and gather where I have not scattered seed? Well then, you should have put my money on deposit with the bankers, so that when I returned I would have received it back with interest. Take the talent from him and give it to the one who has the ten talents. For everyone who has will be given more, and he will have an abundance.

Whoever does not have, even what he has will be taken from him."
—Matthew 25:14-29 NIV

Let's look closer at this passage. The master distributed the talents according to the servants' abilities. This means he considered what the servants could handle and didn't give them more than they could work with. When the master returned, the first servant said that he had taken what had been entrusted to him, sown it, and reaped double the amount. He was so pleased to have an increase to present to the master because he had been privileged to be trusted with the talents in the first place. Likewise with the second servant, who also had an increase to present to the master. But the third servant had an attitude problem. He had the audacity to be manipulative in the midst of his excuse for not doing anything with what he had been given. He told the master that he felt he was a hard master, demanding, unfair, and to be feared. In other words, he said, "It wasn't my fault I did nothing. It was my fear of you that rendered me paralyzed."

It's All in the Way You See It

What was the difference between the three servants? And how does this parable apply to our relationship with God? First things first. The two servants who increased the wealth saw the master in a completely different light than the last servant did. They recognized that they came to the party with nothing. They considered it a privilege to receive the talents and to be trusted with them. They did not look at one another and compare what they had been given, which means they found the master to be fair. They obviously liked the master; they were eager to present him

idolize. This is what wrong thinking does. It leads you to wrong companions who draw you into wrong living. When the consequences of wrong living catch up with you, they solidify your wrong thinking against God. It becomes a vicious cycle. You end up drowning in a sea of self-pity and despair, convinced that God couldn't care less about you. You reason that He's too busy blessing everybody else.

If you are struggling with any of the attitudes I just mentioned, whether they be fleeting thoughts or more repetitive ones, I must ask you this: Do you like God? Is He really your friend? Do you really believe that He is concerned about YOU? Yes, YOU! Not Sally down the street, whose life is always going great. Not John across the way, who always seems to be blessed, no matter what he does. That's a different conversation I won't get into today. Right now we're talking about you. How concerned is He about you? Do you feel as if you are on His mind all of the time? Do you feel as if He is always thinking up special gifts to give you, new ways to show you His love? Do you believe He really takes the time to consider what you can bear? Or have you been saying that you love God merely because it is the right thing to say? Does your heart agree with the confession of your lips? I will ask you again. Do you *like* God?

Be brutally honest with yourself and with Him right now. Pour out your heart to Him about all of your disappointments, all of the things that have caused you to doubt His love for you, and let Him begin to heal those broken places in your heart. Begin to cultivate an attitude of gratitude because, as I've said before, at the end of the day God doesn't owe any one of us anything at all. He already gave us everything in the form of His Son. If He never did another thing for us, what He did from the beginning would be enough. It is a privilege. Better yet, it is by His glorious grace that He chooses to be such a gracious Giver of good things. How does anyone respond to an unexpected gift? They respond with love.

The Three L's

As we choose to change our view of God to that of a loving, considerate suitor, we set the atmosphere for nurturing a love relationship that has great possibilities. Many years ago, when I was new in my walk with Christ, I lived in California for a year. As I prepared to move back to Chicago, I recall my pastor's wife saying to me with deep concern in her tone, "Remember, Michelle, before you marry anyone, make sure you *like* him, you *love* him, and that you are *in love* with him before you say 'I do.' You must have all three to make a marriage work. On the days that you are not in love, at least you will be in like. You will survive then because you share mutual interests in spite of the lack of any chemistry. On the days that you are not in like, your commitment to love will fill the gaps. Being in love will always jump start you back into the other two by introducing a fresh burst of romance into the atmosphere between the two of you." Good advice—advice I remember to this day.

At any rate, there must be a courtship before there can be a wedding. And there must be a wedding before there can be a honeymoon. The courtship is the promise of tomorrow in action. It is the only guide you will have as to what to expect for the rest of your days with the person you are considering marrying. This is the time of cultivating intimacy and building confidence and trust in one another, of establishing habits and personal traditions, of laying the foundation for all of your tomorrows. This is the time for learning all the ins and outs and preferences of one another, deciding once and for all if this is the person you want to be with forever and the way you want to live your life ad infinitum after learning all that you can learn about that person. Well, did you know that Jesus is courting you right now? He has already decided that He wants to spend forever with you!

A wedding is a time of committing to one another, making promises in the presence of witnesses so that you are now accountable to more than just yourself or to one another. Others have heard you promise to have and to hold, for richer or for poorer, in sickness and in health, 'til death do you part, amen. This is not a contract. It is a commitment. It is a commitment that binds two spirits together in an eternal embrace. A contract has time parameters; the promise is only good for as long as the terms of agreement. Aren't you glad God didn't write up a contract to love us until the year 2010, then put in a renewal clause based on our behavior? No, instead He pledges His eternal love to us by His spoken word. Every word that He speaks is true. Why? Because words have life. They are charged with creative energy. Therefore, His promise recreates His love for us afresh every day. This is why His faithfulness is new every morning. The promise of His love to us resounds through the hallowed halls of eternity, recreating and pouring out fresh love daily. We have His commitment, and He requires that we, too, take our vows very seriously.

Do not be quick with your mouth, do not be hasty in your heart to utter anything before God. God is in heaven and you are on earth, so let your words be few. As a dream comes when there are many cares, so the speech of a fool when there are many words. When you make a vow to God, do not delay in fulfilling it. He has no pleasure in fools; fulfill your vow. It is

*better not to vow than to make a vow and not fulfill
it. Do not let your mouth lead you into sin. And do
not protest to the temple messenger, "My vow was a
mistake." Why should God be angry at what you say
and destroy the work of your hands?*
—Ecclesiastes 5:2-6 NIV

Why is breaking a vow considered foolish? Because it
shows that you lacked understanding about what you were
doing in the first place. You did not count the cost of your
commitment. God counted the cost for us, and He paid it
gladly with the death of His Only Begotten Son, Jesus
Christ. He continues to make payments in daily deposits
of faithfulness. Today He asks us to count the cost of loving
Him. Because of all that He has done for us, if we tabulate
our input versus our output, we would have to agree that
it truly costs us nothing to love Him. And we gain so much
in return, more than we will ever be able to repay. God
wants us to fulfill our vow to Him so we can get to the
wedding and get on with the honeymoon.

Getting to the Good Part

Ah, yes, the honeymoon! We all have such romantic
notions about a honeymoon. It is the time of celebrating
our commitment to one another. It is the time when two
friends who have pledged to walk together through life
become lovers, become one. Jesus longs for that oneness
with us. He is looking forward to it. Truly, in His case,
absence makes the heart grow fonder. He is anticipating
receiving His bride and carrying her into His Father's
house. That's us!

---

*In my Father's house are many rooms; if it were not
so, I would have told you. I am going there to prepare
a place for you. And if I go and prepare a place for
you, I will come back and take you to be with me that
you also may be where I am*
——John 14:2, 3 NIV

*Father, I want those you have given me to be with me
where I am...*
——John 17:24 NIV

Can you imagine? Jesus is constantly looking forward
to having us by His side. While we go looking for love in
all the wrong places, there is One standing by who loves us
already. As we go through all kinds of gyrations to win the
love of another human being, there is a Supreme Being
who loves us just the way we are. He knows everything
there is to know about us—the good, the bad, the pretty,
the not-so-pretty, the downright ugly—and He loves us
anyway! Isn't that really the One who wins your heart? The
One who knows you and loves you in spite of yourself?
Who allows you to be you? Who doesn't try to rearrange
you? He embraces you and your imperfections while
loving you to a place that inspires you to be a better you.
That's our fiancé! Jesus is His name! For those who have
suffered the pain of rejection, He extends loving accep-
tance. For those who have experienced the joy of marriage
on earth, He offers you a higher love than what you
already know. For those whose hearts ache, whether single
or married, He Himself will be a place of refuge for your
hurting heart. He longs to love you as no other has loved
you. He Himself will fill those places in your heart that
others have left wanting.

Let the beloved of the LORD *rest secure in him, for he shields him all day long, and the one the* LORD *loves rests between his shoulders*
—Deuteronomy 33:12 NIV, emphasis mine

For your Maker is your husband—the LORD *Almighty is his name—the Holy One of Israel is your Redeemer; he is called the God of all the earth.*
—Isaiah 54:5 NIV

...you will be called by a new name that the mouth of the LORD *will bestow. You will be a crown of splendor in the* LORD'S *hand, a royal diadem in the hand of your God.... For the* LORD *will take delight in you, and your land will be married.... as a bridegroom rejoices over his bride, so will your God rejoice over you.*
—Isaiah 62:2-5 NIV

God rejoices over little ole me! Okay, I know I have to share Him. He rejoices over little ole you, too! We are the beloved! And in His love we have perfect and eternal rest. We don't have to wonder if He loves us. We don't have to sit and play with daisies, chanting, "He loves me, He loves me not, He loves me, He loves me not..." He loves us and that is final. He invites us to snuggle into His bosom and relax in His love.

Always and Forever

As I thought back to the look of complete contentment and peace on Shirley's face as she danced her first official bride's dance with HIM to the strains of "Always," I pondered the words. Stevie Wonder was singing about how his love would last beyond the seasons, beyond the time when night would turn to day, beyond...well, you name it! In other words, he was going to be loving this woman for a long, long time. Longer than any of us could imagine, somewhere beyond eternity. I have to admit that is an overwhelming thought to me...to just love on somebody forever. Whew! Now, that's a lot of lovin'! Yet we can rest assured that the only thing that will remain which is truly important and essential to life is love. Out of all the gifts God gave us, love is the greatest. Why? Because it is the gift of Himself. Now, just stop and think about that. I mean it. Just put this book down and think about that....

From the beginning, God gave you everything pertaining to life and godliness. Then on your birthday He stopped and pondered, "What can I give to someone who already has everything? Hmmm...I know! I will give her Me! Myself! I will lay down My life. That's the best I can do. I hope she likes Me...." Do you like Him? Or do you prefer to be "religious" and play with all the other gifts He has given? The tongues of men and angels, prophecy, teaching, word of knowledge, healing, miracles, helps, administration, apostles, faith, riches.... Guess what? These are all wonderful gifts, but they are like perfume; eventually they will evaporate and be no more. And like any fine fragrance, they can't cover the stench of a cold and loveless heart. A godless heart. So we must remember that God is love personified. Therefore, all you need is God. That is why love is the greatest gift. It is the only thing that will remain along with faith and hope. The only reason faith and hope can remain is because of the presence of God. Without Him, there is no hope and we have nothing to believe in.

Love never fails. But where there are prophecies, they will cease; where there are tongues, they will be stilled; where there is knowledge, it will pass away.
—1 Corinthians 13:8 NIV

...but when perfection comes, the imperfect disappears.
—1 Corinthians 13:10 NIV

And now these three remain: faith, hope and love. But the greatest of these is love.
—1 Corinthians 13:13 NIV

God never fails. His love never fails us. Love is eternal because God is eternal. But we must give all that we are to be able to embrace all that He is. So many times we fall short of truly giving ourselves to God and to others. We throw material gifts and tokens at our friends and loved ones, hoping they will fill the space between us. We gladly give offerings for the latest project at church and hope they make up for the part of ourselves that we withhold from God. We wash our feet and then determine that they are too clean for us to go running into His arms.

I slept but my heart was awake. Listen! My lover is knocking: "Open to me, my sister, my darling, my dove, my flawless one. My head is drenched with dew, my hair with the dampness of the night." I have taken off my robe—must I put it on again? I have washed my feet—must I soil them again? My lover thrust his hand through the latch-opening; my heart began to

> *pound for him. I arose to open for my*
> *lover, and my hands dripped with myrrh, my fingers*
> *with flowing myrrh, on the handles of the lock. I*
> *opened for my lover, but my lover had left; he was*
> *gone. My heart sank at his departure. I looked for him*
> *but did not find him. I called him but he did not*
> *answer. The watchmen found me as they made their*
> *rounds in the city. They beat me, they bruised me;*
> *they took away my cloak, those watchmen of the*
> *walls! O daughters of Jerusalem, I charge you—if you*
> *find my lover, what will you tell him?*
> *Tell him I am faint with love.*
>
> —Song of Songs 5:2-8 NIV

As with the Shulamite, our Bridegroom comes knocking at the door of our heart and we find ourselves unable, sometimes unwilling, to respond. And He, being a perfect gentleman, will not force His affections upon us. The void we feel at His withdrawal causes us to venture into territory that is dangerous. Looking for love where He is not present will always cause us to be wounded. What is it about us? Why do we strain so hard to hold on to the last pieces of ourselves? Why are we so afraid to wholeheartedly give our love to the Lord? What do we think He will do to us if we give ourselves completely? Some of us feel we will turn into some type of crazy fanatic if we allow ourselves to totally surrender to His love. So we run from what we've been seeking all along—true fulfillment, joy, and peace. We only come to this point of realization after leaving ourselves open to others who don't understand the value of our hearts. They drop our hearts and damage them, leaving us disillusioned at the prospect of ever finding a love who will complete us. We find ourselves limping, wounded spirit in hand, back to the arms of the Lord, seeking our soul's restoration. When the Shulamite came to herself and admitted her need for the king, she found herself surrounded by his love. How did she get to this place? By rehearsing all of his goodness to those around her. As she asked her friends to help her find her lover, they asked her the reason for her ardor. And she had a ready answer.

How is your beloved better than others, most beautiful of women? How is your beloved better than others, that you charge us so? My lover is radiant and ruddy, outstanding among ten thousand. His head is purest gold; his hair is wavy and black as a raven. His eyes are like doves by the water streams, washed in milk, mounted like jewels. His cheeks are like beds of spice yielding perfume. His lips are like lilies dripping with myrrh. His arms are rods of gold set with chrysolite. His body is like polished ivory decorated with sapphires. His legs are pillars of marble set on bases of pure gold. His appearance is like Lebanon, choice as its cedars. His mouth is sweetness itself; he is altogether lovely. This is my lover, this my friend, O daughters of Jerusalem. Where has your lover gone, most beautiful of women? Which way did your lover turn, that we may look for him with you?
—Song of Songs 5:9–6:1 NIV

By the time she was finished listing all of her lover's virtues, the other women were ready to seek him, too! After all, who in her right mind wouldn't fall in love with a man like that? That's when you know it's truly love—when it becomes contagious.

On the Love Tip: Last but Certainly Not Least

We, too, have a Love worth talking about. He's not just handsome, He is fine! The Fairest of Ten Thousand! He wears the most costly cologne, the Rose of Sharon. (I believe that's where they got the idea for Joy perfume.) He has the most incredible voice. The most beautiful eyes—deep and endless, filled with love. There is healing in His hands. Now, that's what I call a special touch. He is faithful and true. How divine! He is generous, compassionate, tender, and gracious. He is all-powerful, all-knowing, and His presence is felt everywhere. When He speaks, people listen and do His bidding. Even spirit principalities stand and take notice. And He is so creative! He is a master artiste. His talents are unrivaled. His handiwork is breathtaking. He keeps His promises, He cannot lie. And He is not afraid of commitment! He takes wealth and riches to another level; we're talking deep pockets. The cattle on a thousand hills belong to Him. He loves jewelry, and His property is surrounded by precious jewels. He even has pearly gates! And I hear His mansion is outrageous, with rooms unnumbered and a pure gold driveway! He's promised to take us there. Oh, yes, I think I could get into a Man like that, couldn't you? So stop and take another look at Jesus. Begin to see Him not only as Lord and King, Savior and Deliverer, but as a Real, True Lover of Your Soul.

Begin to picture Him as a real man, your fiancé. Envision the reality of Him though you cannot see His face.

Consider your wedding date with Him a sort of blind date. You've experienced meeting someone on the phone. You've had numerous conversations with him. You like the way he sounds. He's saying all the right things. You are anticipating meeting that man face to face. The anticipation builds. This is the way it should be with our relationship with Christ. But unlike the typical blind date, we will not be disappointed when He appears. He is the romantic fairy tale come to life. The Bible says that He will come on a white horse. He is the original knight in shining armor! No—better yet—He's a king! And if you've never been swept off your feet before, get ready. We will be caught up to meet Him in the air. He will come to carry us away and present us to His Father, who has prepared a magnificent wedding feast for us. We will become one with Him in an eternal embrace. Get ready for the love affair to end all other love affairs. And we will live with Him happily ever after, forever and ever. Amen.

My Dear Beloved,

Know that I have loved you from everlasting to everlasting, and I long for you to be My very own. I know when you sit and when you rise; I perceive your thoughts from afar. I am familiar with all of your ways. Before a word is on your tongue, I know it completely. I hem you in—behind and before; I have laid My hand upon you. You cannot flee from My presence. My goodness and mercy will pursue you all the days of your life. My blessings will overtake you, so determined am I to lavish you with My grace. If you go up to the heavens, I am there; if you make your bed in the depths, I am there. If you rise on the wings of the dawn, if you settle on the far side of the sea, even there My hand will guide you, My right hand will hold you fast. If you say, "Surely the darkness will hide me and the light become night around me," even the darkness will not be dark to Me; the night will shine like the day, for darkness is as light to Me, so powerful is the light of My love for you. For I created your inmost being; I knit you together in your mother's womb. I saw to it that you were fearfully and wonderfully made. Your frame was not hidden from Me when you were made in the secret place. My eyes saw your unformed body. Even then, all the days ordained for you were written in My book before one of them came to be. I made plans for your good and not for evil, to prosper you and give you a determined end by My side. If only you knew how vast the sum of My thoughts were toward you. Then you would know that nothing could ever separate you from My love. Not trouble, not hardship, not persecution, not famine, not nakedness, not danger, nor the sword. Neither death, nor life, angels nor demons, present nor future, nor any powers, height, or depth, or anything that you can imagine—nothing will ever be able to separate you from My love, you have My word.

From My heart to yours,
The One Who Loves You Most